CHINESE CRASH COURSE
速成中文

(第三册)
(Volume 3)

于淼　编著
(By Yu Miao)

北京语言大学出版社
BEIJING LANGUAGE AND CULTURE
UNIVERSITY PRESS

(京)新登字 157 号

图书在版编目(CIP)数据

速成中文/于淼编著.—北京:北京语言大学出版社,
2007.6
ISBN 978-7-5619-1808-1

Ⅰ.速… Ⅱ.于… Ⅲ.汉语-对外汉语教学-教材
Ⅳ.H195.4

中国版本图书馆 CIP 数据核字(2007)第 030869 号

书　　名:	速成中文·3
中文编辑:	周鹂
英文编辑:	武思敏
责任印制:	汪学发
出版发行:	北京语言大学出版社
社　　址:	北京市海淀区学院路 15 号　邮政编码:100083
网　　址:	www.blcup.com
电　　话:	发行部　82303650/3591/3651
	编辑部　82303647
	读者服务部　82303653/3908
印　　刷:	北京新丰印刷厂
经　　销:	全国新华书店
版　　次:	2007 年 8 月第 1 版　2007 年 8 月第 1 次印刷
开　　本:	889 毫米×1194 毫米　1/32　印张:7.5
字　　数:	201 千字　印数:1—5000
书　　号:	ISBN 978-7-5619-1808-1/H·07026

凡有印装质量问题,本社负责调换。电话:82303590

目 录
Contents

第 1 课 Lesson One	汉语热 ············· 1 Chinese craze
第 2 课 Lesson Two	武侠——中国人的成人童话 ······ 14 Chivalrous swordsmen — Chinese adult's fairy tales
第 3 课 Lesson Three	"黄金周"里找黄金 ········ 27 Find gold in the "Golden Week"
第 4 课 Lesson Four	中国人的婚恋观 ········· 40 The Chinese people's notion of love and marriage
第 5 课 Lesson Five	中国人的地方性格 ········ 51 The regional characters of the Chinese people
第 6 课 Lesson Six	关于京剧 ············· 64 About the Beijing opera
第 7 课 Lesson Seven	海外华人 ············· 77 Overseas Chinese

| 第 8 课 | 成语故事(一) | .... | 90 |
| Lesson Nine | Idiom story (1) | | |

| 第 9 课 | 成语故事(二) | .... | 101 |
| Lesson Nine | Idiom story (2) | | |

| 第 10 课 | 一封情书 | .... | 113 |
| Lesson Ten | A love letter | | |

| 第 11 课 | 老太太唱情歌 | .... | 125 |
| Lesson Eleven | The old ladies sing love songs | | |

| 第 12 课 | 爸爸,您能听见吗 | .... | 137 |
| Lesson Twelve | Dad, can you hear me | | |

| 第 13 课 | 中国的流动人口与人口流动 | .... | 148 |
| Lesson Thirteen | Chinese floating population and population flow | | |

| 第 14 课 | 新闻 | .... | 161 |
| Lesson Fourteen | News | | |

| 第 15 课 | 普通话与方言 | .... | 173 |
| Lesson Fifteen | *Putonghua* and dialects | | |

| 生　　词 | New Words | .... | 187 |
| 专有名词 | Proper Nouns | .... | 209 |

Contents

附 录 1 Appendix 1	唐诗五首 ················ Five poems of the Tang Dynasty	211
附 录 2 Appendix 2	谚语八则 ················ Eight proverbs	216
附 录 3 Appendix 3	歇后语六则 ·············· Six two-part allegorical sayings	223
附 录 4 Appendix 4	典故 ···················· Four allusions	229

第 1 课 汉语热
Lesson One Chinese craze

2005年7月20日至22日,首届世界汉语大会在北京召开。据统计,目前海外约有100个国家的2500多所大学有中文课程,通过各种方式学习汉语的人已经超过3000万,"汉语热"正在世界范围内持续升温。

Chinese Crash Course

在德国汉堡市，政府官员每人都有中文名片；汉堡市政府的网站有很多中文网页；汉堡市的街道还有中文路牌。不过，德国的"汉语热"也存在着一些问题，"方块字"是德国学生学习汉语的最大障碍。

目前在美国，讲汉语的人数已经超过讲德语或法语的人。汉语已成为美国第二外语。2003年，美国政府作出决定，把中文作为美国大学的选修课程。

在中国的外国留学生中，韩国学生占大多数。2004年全世界参加HSK考试的人有3.2万，其中韩国人有

Lesson One   Chinese craze

èr diǎn èr wàn.   Zài Tàiguó,   xué Hànyǔ   yě   chéngle   yì zhǒng
2.2   万。在 泰 国，学 汉 语 也 成 了 一 种
shíshàng.
时 尚。

　　　Zài Zhōngguó kuàisù   fāzhǎn   de   jīntiān,   Hànyǔ,
　　在 中 国 快 速 发 展 的 今 天，汉 语，
yǐjīng   bù   jǐn   shǔyú Zhōngguó.
已 经 不 仅 属 于 中 国。

　　The First World Chinese Conference was held in Beijing from the 20th to 22nd of July, 2005. According to the statistics, there are more than 2,500 universities that have Chinese courses in 100 foreign countries or so at present. There are more than 30 million people studying Chinese by various means, and the "Chinese craze" is heating up worldwide.

　　In the city of Hamburg, Germany, every government official has a business card in Chinese. The government's official website has many webpages in Chinese. It also has street nameplates Chinese. But there are also some problems with the Chinese craze in Germany: Square-shaped Chinese characters are the biggest impediment in the process of learning Chinese among the German students.

　　In the United States, the number of people that speak Chinese now exceeds the number that speaks German or French. Chinese has become the second foreign language of America. The American government has made decision that Chinese

should be offered as an elective course in the American universities.

Among the foreign students in China, the South Korean students account for the bulk. There were 32 thousand people who took the HSK test in 2004. Among them 22 thousand were South Korean people. It has also become a fashion to learn Chinese in Thailand.

China is developing with a high speed now. The Chinese language does not only belong to China.

生 词 New Words

1. 至	zhì	(动)	to
2. 首届	shǒujiè	(数量)	first session
首	shǒu		first
3. 召开	zhàokāi	(动)	hold
4. 据	jù	(介)	according to
5. 统计	tǒngjì	(动)	statistics
6. 海外	hǎiwài	(名)	overseas
7. 约/大约	yuē/dàyuē	(副)	about
8. 超过	chāoguò	(动)	exceed

Lesson One　Chinese craze

9. 范围	fànwéi	(名)	scope
10. 内	nèi	(名)	inside
11. 持续	chíxù	(动)	continue
12. 升温	shēngwēn	(动)	increase in temperature
13. 官员	guānyuán	(名)	official
14. 网站	wǎngzhàn	(名)	website
15. 网页	wǎngyè	(名)	webpage
16. 街道	jiēdào	(名)	street
17. 路牌	lùpái	(名)	street nameplate
18. 不过	búguò	(连)	but
19. 存在	cúnzài	(动)	exist
20. 方块字	fāngkuàizì	(名)	(square-shaped) Chinese character
21. 障碍	zhàng'ài	(名)	impediment
22. 作为	zuòwéi	(动)	act as
23. 选修	xuǎnxiū	(动)	take as an elective (course)
24. 占	zhàn	(动)	account for
25. 其中	qízhōng	(名)	within
26. 时尚	shíshàng	(名、形)	fashion; fashionable
27. 快速	kuàisù	(形)	quick
28. 属于	shǔyú	(动)	belong to

Chinese Crash Course

 **Proper Nouns**

1. 德国	Déguó	Germany
2. 汉堡市	Hànbǎo Shì	Hamburg (City)
3. 德语	Déyǔ	German
4. 法语	Fǎyǔ	French
5. 韩国	Hánguó	South Korea
6. 泰国	Tàiguó	Thailand

 **Sentence Patterns**

1. ……在……召开

首届世界汉语大会在北京召开。

The First World Chinese Conference was held in Beijing.

2003年,第三届汽车技术研讨会在北京召开。

The Third Auto Technology Seminar was held in Beijing in 2003.

2. 据统计,……

据统计,目前海外约有2500多所大学有中文课程。

According to the statistics, there are more than 2,500 overseas universities that have Chinese courses at present.

Lesson One　Chinese craze

据统计,每年有30万游客到这里观光旅游。

According to the statistics, there are 300 thousand tourists that come here for sightseeing and touring each year.

3. 在……范围内

"汉语热"正在世界范围内持续升温。

The "Chinese craze" is heating up worldwide.

在全国范围内,一共有7所大学开设了这门课程。

There are a total of seven universities setting up this course nationwide.

4. ……,不过,……

不过,德国的"汉语热"也存在着一些问题。

But there are also some problems with the Chinese craze in Germany.

这个美国人汉语说得很流利,不过,他不会写汉字。

This American speaks Chinese very fluently, but he can't write Chinese.

5. ……存在着……

德国的"汉语热"也存在着一些问题。

There are also some problems with the Chinese craze in Germany.

这个合同里存在着很多问题。

There are many problems in this contract.

Chinese Crash Course

6. 把……作为……

美国政府作出决定,把中文作为美国大学的选修课程。

The American government has decided to make Chinese an elective course in American universities.

让我们把这次活动作为我们合作的开始。

Let's make this activity as the beginning of our cooperation.

7. 在……中,……占多数

在中国的外国留学生中,韩国学生占大多数。

Among the foreign students in China, the South Korean students account for the bulk.

在这些病人中,发烧的占多数。

Among these patients, the people with fevers account for the bulk.

通过各种方式学习汉语的人

tōngguò gè zhǒng fāngshì xuéxí Hànyǔ de rén

"通过"在这里是介词,引进动作的媒介或手段。例如:

"Tōngguò" is a preposition introducing the means or vehicle of an action. For example:

通过学习中国文化,我更了解中国了。

I know more about China by learning Chinese culture.

Lesson One Chinese craze

通过朋友的介绍,我认识了她。
I know her through my friend's introduction.
我们通过什么方式才能很好地交流呢?
By what manner can we communicate well?

 练 习 Exercises

一 根据课文完成词语搭配 Complete the following word-collocations according to the text.

召开(　　)　　　存在(　　)　　　(　　)的障碍
快速(　　)　　　(　　)范围　　　(　　)网页

二 选择填空 Choose the correct answers.

1. 这首歌很快在全国范围(　　)流行起来。
   A 外　　　B 中　　　C 内　　　D 下
2. 他的水平已经(　　)了他的老师。
   A 经过　　B 通过　　C 高　　　D 超过
3. 很多外国人把汉语(　　)一门重要的外语来学习。
   A 成为　　B 作为　　C 是　　　D 以为
4. (　　)统计,2004年全世界有三万多人参加了汉语水平考试。
   A 看　　　B 来　　　C 做　　　D 据

Chinese Crash Course

 模仿句型造句　Make sentences with the given sentence patterns.

1. 在……范围内

2. 在……中,……占多数

3. ……存在着

相关阅读
Related Reading

(一)

　　Měiguó xué Zhōngwén de rénshù chíxù zēngduō yǒu yǐxià
　　美　国　学　中　文　的　人　数　持续　增多　有　以下
jǐ ge yuányīn: dì yī, xǔduō Měiguórén xīwàng tōngguò
几 个 原 因：第一，许多 美国人 希望 通过
Zhōngwén jiāshēn duì Zhōngguó de liǎojiě; dì èr, mùqián
中　文　加深　对　中　国　的　了解；第二，目前
Měi Zhōng jīngjì màoyì guānxi fāzhǎn hěn kuài, zài Měiguó yuè
美　中　经济　贸易　关系　发展　很　快，在　美国　越
lái yuè duō gōngzuò gǎngwèi xūyào shǐyòng Zhōngwén;
来 越 多 工 作 岗 位 需要 使用 中文；
xǔduō Měiguórén xīwàng tōngguò xué Zhōngwén, lái gèng hǎo de
许多　美国人　希望　通过　学　中文，来　更　好　地

Lesson One　Chinese craze

和中国人做生意；第三，中国目前的经济发展很快，生活条件大大改善，许多美国学生希望学好中文，将来到中国求发展；第四，越来越多的美国华人希望自己的孩子能学好中文，并能了解中国传统文化，为将来到中国发展作好准备。

根据阅读内容判断正误：

1. 美国学生学习中文是为了考试升学。　　　　（　　）
2. 美国人学习中文都是为了了解中国文化。　　（　　）
3. 中国的经济发展引发了很多美国人学习汉语的兴趣。（　　）

（二）

来自中国国家汉语国际推广领导小组办公室（简称"国家汉办"）的信息表明，目前在全球存在着对汉语的强劲需求，而由此形成的汉语教师短缺的情况也格外醒目。

Chinese Crash Course

让我们看看国家汉办提供的数字：马来西亚汉语教师缺口9万，印度尼西亚缺口10万。汉办主任解释说，这些数字都是教育访问团出访时对方国家提出的。

据有关人士介绍，日本、韩国、泰国、菲律宾、越南、印尼、中亚五国、印度、巴基斯坦等周边国家对汉语教师的需求都非常迫切；非洲、阿拉伯地区、南美也有要求；而欧洲、北美、澳大利亚、新西兰等发达国家也都希望在汉语教师方面得到中国的帮助。

"汉语教师需求倍增，汉语教学持续、快速发展，传统和常规的办法已难以满足这个要求。"教育部副部长

Lesson One Chinese craze

章新胜说。在这个背景下,"国际汉语教师志愿者计划"应运而生。国家汉办为此设立了国际汉语教师中国志愿者中心,负责志愿者的招聘、培训、派出、签约、咨询、经费支持以及日常管理等具体事务。据悉,目前国家汉办网站注册报名的点击量已超过3万次。

根据阅读内容判断正误:

1. 国际上对外汉语教师数量明显不够。　　　　（　）
2. 中国政府启动了专业汉语教师大量出国教学的计划。（　）
3. 在韩国,汉语教师的数量是充足的。　　　　（　）

第 2 课 武侠——中国人的成人童话

Lesson Two Chivalrous swordsmen — Chinese adult's fairy tales

在中国，武侠是一种很有趣的文化现象，大部分中国人都读过武侠小说，很多人还是武侠迷。为什么会形成这种现象呢？原因是很复杂的。武侠至少有两千年的历史了，他们不但勇敢，而且有自己的人生理想，他们为了正义可以献出自己的生命。儒家和道家的思想构成了武侠的性格。儒家思想使他们有正义感和责任感，而道家思想使他们喜欢自由地

Lesson Two　Chivalrous swordsmen — Chinese adult's fairy tales

生活。武侠的世界也叫"江湖","江湖"里是没有法律和政府的,但是,"江湖"里有道德,法律不能解决的问题,武侠可以用自己的行为方式来解决。

中国是武侠电影的故乡,武侠片常常有相似的情节,但是中国人还是百看不厌。童话是简单的,可是我们还是给孩子们一遍一遍地讲下去。

Chinese Crash Course

Wǔxiá wénhuà bāohánle Zhōngguórén de lìshǐ、jīngshén
武侠文化包含了中国人的历史、精神
hé chuántǒng, suǒyǐ shuō, wǔxiá jiù chéngle Zhōngguórén de
和传统，所以说，武侠就成了中国人的
chéngréntónghuà。
成人童话。

The chivalrous swordsmen are a very interesting cultural phenomenon in China. Most Chinese have read novels about the chivalrous swordsmen, and many people are fans of them. What is the reason behind this phenomenon? It is complicated. The history of the chivalrous swordsmen is at least two thousand years old. The people named by the chivalrous swordsmen are not only brave but also have their own ideals. They can devote their lives to justice.

The thinking of Confucianism and Taoism constitutes the characteristics of the chivalrous swordsmen. The thinking of Confucianism made them have a sense of justice and responsibility to others and the thinking of Taoism made them lead a free and casual life. The world of swordsmen is also called "*jianghu*". There weren't laws and government in the "*jianghu*", but there were morals in it. When there were problems that couldn't be solved by law, the chivalrous swordsmen could solve them by their own ways.

China is a homeland of swordsman films. Though the

Lesson Two Chivalrous swordsmen — Chinese adult's fairy tales

swordsman films are always similar in plots, Chinese still like to watch them tirelessly. The fairy tales are simple but we still tell them to the children time and again. The swordsman culture includes the history, spirit and tradition of the Chinese people. So we can say that chivalrous swordsmen are the adult's fairy tales of the Chinese people.

生 词 New Words

1.	武侠	wǔxiá	（名）	chivalrous swordsman
	武	wǔ		martial arts
	侠	xiá		chivalrous man
2.	成人	chéngrén	（名）	adult
3.	童话	tónghuà	（名）	fairy tale
4.	有趣	yǒuqù	（形）	interesting
5.	现象	xiànxiàng	（名）	phenomenon
6.	部分	bùfen	（名）	part
7.	读	dú	（动）	read
8.	小说	xiǎoshuō	（名）	novel
9.	形成	xíngchéng	（动）	become
10.	复杂	fùzá	（形）	complicated
11.	勇敢	yǒnggǎn	（形）	brave

Chinese Crash Course

12. 人生	rénshēng	（名）	life	
13. 理想	lǐxiǎng	（名、形）	ideal; ideal	
14. 正义	zhèngyì	（名）	justice	
15. 献出	xiànchū	（动）	sacrifice	
16. 生命	shēngmìng	（名）	life	
17. 儒家	Rújiā	（名）	Confucianist	
18. 道家	Dàojiā	（名）	Taoist	
19. 思想	sīxiǎng	（名）	thinking	
20. 构成	gòuchéng	（动）	constitute	
21. 而	ér	（连）	but	
22. 法律	fǎlǜ	（名）	law	
23. 道德	dàodé	（名）	moral	
24. 行为	xíngwéi	（名）	behavior	
25. 故乡	gùxiāng	（名）	hometown	
26. 相似	xiāngsì	（形）	similar	
27. 情节	qíngjié	（名）	plot	
28. 百看不厌	bǎi kàn bú yàn		be worth watching a hundred times	
29. 孩子	háizi	（名）	child	
30. 遍	biàn	（量）	(measure word) time	
31. 讲	jiǎng	（动）	tell	
32. 包含	bāohán	（动）	include	
33. 精神	jīngshén	（名）	spirit	

Lesson Two Chivalrous swordsmen — Chinese adult's fairy tales

句 型 Sentence Patterns

1. ……形成……

为什么会形成这种现象呢？

What is the reason behind this phenomenon?

南方文化和北方文化在这里融合，慢慢形成了一种新的文化形态。

The culture of South and North integrated here, becoming a new cultural form gradually.

2. 不但……，而且……

他们不但勇敢，而且有自己的人生理想。

They are not only brave but also have their own ideals.

这种汽车不但质量好，而且价格也便宜。

This kind of car not only has a good quality but also has a cheap price.

3. 用……方式……

法律不能解决的问题，武侠可以用自己的行为方式来解决。

When there were problems that couldn't be solved by law, the chivalrous swordsmen could solve them by their own ways.

我们用好朋友的方式跟他交流。

We communicated with him by the manner of a good friend.

Chinese Crash Course

4. 一遍一遍地……

童话是简单的,可是我们还是给孩子们一遍一遍地讲下去。

The fairy tales are simple but we still tell them to the children time and again.

他太喜欢这首歌了,一个下午他在房间里一遍一遍地听。

He liked this song very much and listened to it again and again in the room for a whole afternoon.

5. ……包含……

武侠文化包含了中国人的历史、精神和传统。

The swordsmen culture includes the history, spirit and tradition of the Chinese people.

京剧里包含了中国人的忠孝节义、礼乐教化。

Beijing opera includes the loyalty and filial piety, integrity and justice, courtesy, music and civilization of the Chinese people.

注 释 Annotations

1. 百看不厌   *bǎi kàn bú yàn*

表示因为特别喜欢而反复地欣赏,也可以说"*bǎi tīng bú yàn*"。例如:

This structure indicates to appreciate something again and again because one likes it very much. We can also say "*bǎi tīng bú yàn*".

Lesson Two Chivalrous swordsmen — Chinese adult's fairy tales

For example:

这么优美的民歌真是百听不厌。

Such graceful folk song are worth hearing for many times.

有一些老电影对中国人来说是百看不厌的。

Some old films are enjoyed by the Chinese people tirelessly.

2. 一遍一遍地　　*yí biàn yí biàn de*

这种动量词或者名量词的重叠表示反复、重复、连续或全部的意思。例如：

The reduplication of measure word for action or noun indicates repetition, continuation or the whole. For example:

欢呼声和掌声一阵一阵地响起，演员们一遍一遍地出来谢幕，这种场面真感人。

Acclamation and applause rang out by fits and starts, the actors came out and answered to a curtain call again and again. This scene moved us very much.

前面的人一个一个地倒下，后面的人再一个一个地冲上去。

The people in the front fall down one by one and the people in the back rush to the front again.

我们班的女同学个个都很漂亮。

Every girl in our class is very beautiful.

她把那些照片一张一张地摆出来，然后一张一张地讲述起来。

She placed those photos one by one then spoke of them one after another.

车一辆一辆地开过去，时间也一分一分地过去了。

Cars drove by one by one, and the time passed one minute after another.

练习 Exercises

一 根据课文完成词语搭配 Complete the following word-collocations according to the text.

自由地（　　）　　复杂的（　　）　　人生（　　）
（　　）小说　　　献出（　　）　　（　　）思想
解决（　　）　　（　　）的故乡　　（　　）的情节

二 选择填空 Choose the correct answers.

1. 大部分中国人都（　　）武侠小说。
   A 读了　　　B 读到　　　C 读着　　　D 读过
2. 儒家的思想（　　）武侠有正义感和责任感。
   A 给　　　　B 把　　　　C 被　　　　D 使
3. 武侠电影常常有（　　）的情节。
   A 互相　　　B 相同　　　C 相反　　　D 相似
4. 这首歌他唱了很多（　　）。
   A 个　　　　B 下　　　　C 遍　　　　D 一遍

三 模仿句型造句 Make sentences with the given sentence patterns.

1. ……形成……

Lesson Two Chivalrous swordsmen — Chinese adult's fairy tales

2. 不但……,而且……

3. 用……方式……

相关阅读
Related Reading

（一）

香港的金庸先生是中国当代最有名的武侠小说家。有人说,只要有中国人的地方,就有邓丽君的歌曲和金庸的武侠小说,连邓小平先生也是他的小说迷。

有人统计过,金庸的小说从上个世纪70年代到现在大约出版了三亿册。他的大多数作品被改编成了电影和电视连续剧,如《神雕侠侣》和

"Xiào Ào Jiānghú", dōu bèi pāichéngle bù tóng bǎnběn
《笑傲江湖》，都被拍成了不同版本
de yǐngshì zuòpǐn. Nǐ xiànzài dǎkāi diànshì, yěxǔ
的影视作品。你现在打开电视，也许
jiù huì kàndào gēnjù Jīn Yōng xiǎoshuō gǎibiān de
就会看到根据金庸小说改编的
diànshìjù ne!
电视剧呢!

根据阅读内容判断正误：

1. 金庸先生写了很多武侠电视剧剧本。　　（　）
2. 邓小平先生也喜欢金庸先生的作品。　　（　）
3. 现在没有人喜欢武侠小说了。　　　　　（　）

（二）

"Xīn wǔxiá xīn wénhuà" xìliè dònghuà diànyǐng zuò-
"新武侠新文化"系列动画电影作
wéi zhěngtǐ xiàngmù, mùqián yǐjīng shēnbào guójiā "shíyī wǔ"
为整体项目，目前已经申报国家"十一五"
guīhuà. Dì yī pī shí bù chángpiān wǔxiá dònghuà diànyǐng
规划。第一批10部长篇武侠动画电影
tícái, jiāng zài jìnqī tōngguò hùliánwǎng, miànxiàng
题材，将在近期通过互联网，面向
quánqiú, yóu Zhōngguó wǔxiá wénhuà àihàozhě hé zhùmíng
全球，由中国武侠文化爱好者和著名
wǔxiá wénhuà zhuānjiā gòngtóng xuǎnchū, ránhòu shàng-
武侠文化专家共同选出，然后上

Lesson Two Chivalrous swordsmen — Chinese adult's fairy tales

报国家电影局审批立项。第一部武侠动画电影最迟将于2006年3月前开拍。10部动画电影总投资约为6亿元人民币。

　　漫画版金庸作品即将面世了！日前，《天龙八部》作为首部改编成漫画的作品，已经开始面向全国招募漫画脚本创作者。据悉，《天龙八部》系列由24本漫画组成，每页有漫画3至4幅，文字50个左右。除了《天龙八部》以外，还将在三年内完成其他三部金庸作品的漫画改编，分别是：《神雕侠侣》、《倚天屠龙记》和《笑傲江湖》。这4部成功完成之后，金庸的其他作品也将陆续被改编成漫画作品。

Chinese Crash Course

根据阅读内容判断正误：

1. 武侠动画电影的拍摄与政府无关。　　　　（　　）

2. 漫画版的金庸作品已经上市了。　　　　　（　　）

3. 金庸作品只有4部被改编成漫画版。　　　（　　）

第3课 "黄金周"里找黄金
Lesson Three Find gold in the "Golden Week"

从1999年开始,中国政府把五月一日的国际劳动节、十月一日的国庆节和春节等三个假期都延长到了七天,从此,中国人就有了"黄金周",这样全年的法定假日一共是120天左右。

有时候"十一黄金周"还正好赶上

Chinese Crash Course

chuántǒng jiérì Zhōngqiū Jié ne!
传统节日中秋节呢!

Zěnme dùguò huángjīnzhōu, chéngle Zhōngguórén
怎么度过黄金周,成了中国人
měi nián yào kǎolǜ de jiāodiǎn wèntí, zhème cháng de
每年要考虑的焦点问题,这么长的
jiàqī ràng Zhōngguórén yòu xīngfèn yòu tóuténg. Xīngfèn
假期让中国人又兴奋又头疼。兴奋
de shì kěyǐ yǒu shíjiān hǎohāor fàngsōng zìjǐ, tóuténg
的是可以有时间好好儿放松自己,头疼
de shì bù zhīdao xuǎnzé shénme fāngshì dùjià shì zuì yǒu
的是不知道选择什么方式度假是最有
yìyì de. Qián jǐ nián, hěn duō rén xuǎnzé lǚyóu, kěshì
意义的。前几年,很多人选择旅游,可是
nàme duō Zhōngguórén dōu lǚxíng, jiāotōng hé shí sù jiù
那么多中国人都旅行,交通和食宿就
bù fāngbiàn le. Xiànzài Zhōngguó de chéngshì jūmín
不方便了。现在中国的城市居民
fāxiàn, lǚyóu bìng bú shì tāmen wéiyī de xuǎnzé, zuì
发现,旅游并不是他们唯一的选择,最
zhòngyào de shì zài jiàqī li zhǎodào zìjǐ zuì yǒu
重要的是在假期里找到自己最有
jiàzhí de dōngxi hé zuì kuàilè de dōngxi, rénmen de
价值的东西和最快乐的东西,人们的
jiàrì xiāofèi guānniàn yě zhèngzài fāshēng gǎibiàn. Yǒu rén
假日消费观念也正在发生改变。有人
lìyòng jiàqī xuéxí jìshù, yǒu rén lìyòng jiàqī hé
利用假期学习技术,有人利用假期和

Lesson Three Find gold in the "Golden Week"

家人团聚,有人利用假期购买汽车或看房地产市场,还有人喜欢在图书馆里看书。因为这些都是平时没时间做的事情。

中国人都说,在"黄金周"里要找黄金,就是找自己的健康、时尚、有意义的生活。那么,你在中国的下一个"黄金周"会怎么过呢?

Since 1999, the Chinese government has extended the holiday period of the Labor Day, National Day and Spring Festival to seven days. From then on, Chinese people began to have their "Golden Weeks". Then the legal holiday is altogether 120 days or so in a year. Sometimes the "Golden Weeks" of the National Day just coincide with the traditional Mid-Autumn Festival.

How to spend the Golden Weeks has become the focus which the Chinese people think about every year. The long holiday period make the Chinese feel both excited and

Chinese Crash Course

headachy. They are excited because they have time to relax. They get a headache because they don't know how to spend the most wonderful holiday. Several years ago, most people chose to travel. However, the traffic, board and lodging were inconvenient when most of the Chinese people did so at the same time. Now the townsmen in China find that traveling is not the only choice for them. To find the most valuable and happiest thing in the holiday is particularly important. People's holiday consumption concepts are also changing. Some people use the holiday to learn skills, some to unite with their families, some to purchase autos or go to see model home and some to read books in the library. Because all of these things you can't do in ordinary times as you don't have the vacant hours.

All the Chinese say they would search for gold in the "Golden Week". It just means that they want to search for health, fashion and a meaningful life. How would you spend the next "Golden Week" in China?

生 词　New Words

1. 黄金　　　huángjīn　　（名）　　gold
2. 劳动　　　láodòng　　（动）　　labor

Lesson Three　Find gold in the "Golden Week"

3. 节/节日	jié/jiérì	（名）		festival
4. 国庆	guóqìng	（名）		National Day
5. 等	děng	（助）		etc.
6. 延长	yáncháng	（动）		extend
7. 此	cǐ	（代）		this
8. 法定	fǎdìng	（形）		legal
9. 假日	jiàrì	（名）		holiday
10. 一共	yígòng	（副）		altogether
11. 有时候	yǒushíhou	（副）		sometimes
12. 赶上	gǎnshang	（动）		catch up with
13. 度过	dùguò	（动）		spend
14. 焦点	jiāodiǎn	（名）		focus
15. 放松	fàngsōng	（动）		relax
16. 有意义	yǒu yìyì			meaningful
意义	yìyì	（名）		meaning
17. 交通	jiāotōng	（名）		traffic
18. 食宿	shí sù			board and lodging
19. 居民	jūmín	（名）		resident
20. 并	bìng	（副）		together
21. 唯一	wéiyī	（形）		only
22. 价值	jiàzhí	（名）		value
23. 观念	guānniàn	（名）		concept
24. 利用	lìyòng	（动）		use

Chinese Crash Course

25. 团聚	tuánjù	（动）	unite
26. 房地产	fángdìchǎn	（名）	real estate
27. 健康	jiànkāng	（名、形）	health; healthy

专有名词　Proper Nouns

1. 五一国际劳动节　Wǔ-Yī Guójì Láodòng Jié　May Day
2. 十一国庆节　Shí-Yī Guóqìng Jié　National Day of October First
3. 春节　Chūn Jié　Spring Festival
4. 中秋节　Zhōngqiū Jié　Mid-Autumn Festival

句　型　Sentence Patterns

1. ……延长……

中国政府把三个假日都延长到了七天。

The Chinese government has extended all the three holidays to seven days.

会议的时间延长了两天。

The meeting was prolonged for two days.

Lesson Three Find gold in the "Golden Week"

2. 从此……

从此,中国人就有了"黄金周"。

From then on, Chinese people began to have their "Golden Weeks".

他们终于结婚了,从此,他们过上了幸福的生活。

They got married eventually. From then on, they led a happy life.

3. 正好赶上……

"十一黄金周"有时正好赶上传统节日中秋节。

The "Golden Weeks" of the National Day just coincide with the traditional Mid-Autumn Festival.

我跑到地铁站,正好赶上了最后一班地铁。

I ran to the subway station and fortunately caught the last subway.

4. ……让……

这么长的假期让中国人又兴奋又头疼。

The long holiday makes the Chinese feel both excited and headachy.

这个消息让我很高兴。

This news made me very pleased.

5. 又……又……

假期让中国人又兴奋又头疼。

Holidays make the Chinese feel both excited and headachy.

终于到我表演了,我又兴奋又紧张。

Finally, it was my turn to perform; I felt both excited and nervous.

Chinese Crash Course

6. 好好儿……

终于可以有时间好好儿放松自己了。

Finally, I have time to relax.

今天太累了,我要好好儿睡一觉。

I'm too tired today. I need to have a good sleep.

7. ……并不是……

旅游并不是他们唯一的选择。

Traveling is not the only choice for them.

并不是所有的人都喜欢武侠小说。

Not everyone likes swordsman fiction.

8. 利用……

有人利用假期学习技术,有人利用假期和家人团聚。

Some people use the holiday to learn skills, some to unite with their families.

我要利用这段时间学习汉语。

I want to use this period of time to study Chinese.

注 释 Annotations

1. 从此 *cóngcǐ*

"此"是代词,代替前面提到的事情。还有"因此""此时""此事"等。例如:

Lesson Three Find gold in the "Golden Week"

"Cǐ" is a pronoun. It substitutes the thing that is mentioned before it. There are also "yīncǐ", "cǐ shí", "cǐ shì", etc. For example:

战争已经开始了,此时,他们还在睡觉,根本不知道。

The war has already begun. At that time they were sleeping and didn't know at all.

他的儿子出生了,从此,他就要承担一个父亲的责任了。

His son was born. From then on, he began to take the responsibility of a father.

2. 好好儿放松   *hǎohāor fàngsōng*

"好好儿"在这里是副词,指完全地、程度高地。例如:

"Hǎohāor" is an adverb here, indicating completeness or a high level. For example:

我要好好儿研究这本书。

I will have an in-depth research into this book.

今天我们要好好儿玩一下。

We will have a lot of fun today.

 练 习 Exercises

一 根据课文完成词语搭配 Complete the following word-collocations according to the text.

法定(　　　)　　(　　　)的节日　　放松(　　　)

Chinese Crash Course

(　　)的选择　　　(　　)的东西　　　(　　)观念
购买(　　)　　　利用(　　)　　　(　　)的生活

二　选择填空　Choose the correct answers.

1. 这个会议延长(　)下星期二。
   A 了　　　B 过　　　C 是　　　D 到

2. 这么好的机会我没有(　　)，真遗憾！
   A 赶快　　B 赶忙　　C 赶到　　D 赶上

3. 我(　)不知道这件事情很重要。
   A 没　　　B 很　　　C 非常　　D 并

4. 这是你(　　)的选择，你没有别的办法。
   A 只有　　B 一个　　C 唯一　　D 只要

5. 你要(　　)你的假期？
   A 什么过　B 哪里过　C 怎么过　D 度过

三　模仿句型造句　Make sentences with the given sentence patterns.

1. 又……又……

2. 让……

3. 利用……

Lesson Three Find gold in the "Golden Week"

相关阅读
Related Reading

据统计，2001年的三个"黄金周"里，国内旅游的人数达到1.8亿人次，境外旅游者也逐年增加。旅游收入使中国的GDP增加了一个百分点，这是让人难以相信的惊喜。假日里，图书市场、汽车市场、房地产市场都火了起来，商场还有主题销售活动，所有商家都不会错过"黄金周"的好机会，对他们来说，是"一寸光阴一寸金"。政府说：老百姓休息了，国家变富了，这就是假日经济。

根据阅读内容判断正误：

1. 2001年的三个黄金周,国内外旅游人数共1.8亿人次。（ ）
2. 人们会在黄金周里购买汽车或房子。（ ）
3. 商场在黄金周时会休息,因为假期难得。（ ）

Chinese Crash Course

(二)

2004年"十一黄金周"期间,北京共接待国内游客约425万人次全市公园和市级以上风景名胜区共接待游人670余万人次,旅游总收入为33.2亿元人民币,其中北京市民在京旅游消费达3.5亿元,同比增长55%。

此次"黄金周"故宫游人达到40万人次,是历次"十一黄金周"的最高值,仅次于火爆的2000年和2001年的"五一"。

据河南旅游部门有关人士分析,黄金周期间,该省共接待入境游客1.5万人次,较去年同期增长12.5%。

Lesson Three Find gold in the "Golden Week"

另外，2004年"十一黄金周"期间，河南除了传统的观光旅游外，山水游、文化游、休闲游、近郊游、乡村游、体验游均有增长，客源分布趋于合理，消费理念趋于成熟。

根据阅读内容判断正误：

1. 2000年的"十一"故宫游人数量最多。　　　　（　　）
2. 河南省的旅游项目主要是观光旅游。　　　　（　　）
3. 北京2004年黄金周旅游收入为3亿多人民币。（　　）

第4课 中国人的婚恋观
Lesson Four The Chinese people's notion of love and marriage

中国人传统的恋爱、婚姻观念有的已经成了成语,比如,有"郎才女貌",有"才子佳人",有"门当户对"等等;还有的表现了中国人崇尚的美好品德,如"相敬如宾""白头偕老"等。

Lesson Four The Chinese people's notion of love and marriage

新中国成立后,自由恋爱成了时尚,但是当时的爱情受政治的影响。有人开玩笑地说:"姑娘们60年代喜欢找工人,70年代想嫁给军人。"改革开放后,经济生活改变了中国人的价值观念,中国的年轻人在爱情上积极,在婚姻中平等,但是也有人说,只要过程,不要结果。

现在婚前同居的情况也很多,"网恋"也存在。虽然离婚率不断增高,还有很多人把爱情当做商品,但是大部分人还是珍惜纯洁、美好的爱情的。

爱情是人类最美好的情感之一,中国人在这方面的情感是很复杂的,

kěyǐ　　shuō shì　jì　xiànshí,　yòu làngmàn.
可 以 说 是 既 现 实, 又 浪 漫。

Some traditional notions of Chinese love and marriage have become idioms. Such as, "man's ability matching woman's beauty", "talented scholars matching beautiful ladies", "people should be matched for marriage", etc. Some also express Chinese good virtues praised by Chinese people, for instance: "respecting each other as if the other were a guest" and "living to old age in conjugal bliss".

After the founding of New China, free courtship became a fashion. But the love of that time also was influenced by the politics. Some people said it as a joke: "Girls would like to marry workers in the 1960's and to marry armymen in the 1970's." After the reform and opening to the outside world, the economic development has changed Chinese people's values. The Chinese youth are active in love, and pursue equality in the marriage. But there is also a saying that: "We want only the process not the result."

There are many people cohabiting before marriage, and cyber romance exists too. Although the divorce rate is increasingly high, there are some people who take love as merchandise, most people still think love is the most beautiful and purest thing.

Love is one of the nicest emotions of human beings. Chinese

Lesson Four   The Chinese people's notion of love and marriage

people's feelings towards love are very complicated. It can be said that it is both practical and romantic.

 **New Words**

1. 婚姻	hūnyīn	（名）	marriage
2. 成语	chéngyǔ	（名）	idiom
3. 郎才女貌	láng cái nǔ mào		man has ability and woman has good looks
4. 才子佳人	cáizǐ jiārén		talented scholars and beautiful ladies
5. 门当户对	mén dāng hù duì		be well-matched in social status
6. 表现	biǎoxiàn	（动、名）	represent; representation
7. 品德	pǐndé	（名）	moral character
8. 相敬如宾	xiāng jìng rú bīn		respect each other as if the other were a guest
9. 白头偕老	báitóu xié lǎo		live to old age in conjugal bliss
10. 成立	chénglì	（动）	found
11. 政治	zhèngzhì	（名）	politics
12. 开玩笑	kāi wánxiào		make a joke
玩笑	wánxiào	（名）	joke

Chinese Crash Course

13. 工人	gōngrén	(名)	worker
14. 嫁	jià	(动)	marry
15. 军人	jūnrén	(名)	soldier
16. 改革	gǎigé	(动)	reform
17. 开放	kāifàng	(动、形)	open; open
18. 积极	jījí	(形)	active
19. 平等	píngděng	(形)	equal
20. 过程	guòchéng	(名)	process
21. 同居	tóngjū	(动)	cohabit
22. 离婚	lí//hūn	(动)	divorce
23. 率	lǜ	(名)	rate
24. 纯洁	chúnjié	(形)	pure
25. 情感	qínggǎn	(名)	emotion
26. ……之一	……zhī yī		one of...
27. 现实	xiànshí	(名、形)	reality; realistic
28. 浪漫	làngmàn	(形)	romantic

 **Sentence Patterns**

1. ……表现……

"相敬如宾""白头偕老"表现了中国人崇尚的美好品德。

"Respecting each other as if the other were a guest" and "living

Lesson Four The Chinese people's notion of love and marriage

to old age in conjugal bliss", express a good moral character praised by the Chinese people.

这场比赛表现出了我们的水平。

This match showed our level.

2. 受……影响

当时的爱情受政治的影响。

The love of that time was influenced by the politics.

地域文化也受地理环境的影响。

A regional culture is also influenced by the geographical environment.

3. ……率

现在的离婚率很高。

The divorce rate is very high now.

这批产品的合格率很低。

The acceptance rate of this batch of products is very low.

4. ……之一

爱情是人类最美好的情感之一。

Love is one of the nicest emotions of human beings.

搜狐网是中国最大的网站之一。

Sohu is one of the largest websites in China.

注 释　Annotations

1. 受(影响)　　*shòu (yǐngxiǎng)*

"受"表示接受或遭受,可以带动词做宾语,也可以接兼语。例如:

"Shòu" indicates accepting or suffering. It can take a verb as an object and also can be followed by a pivot. For example:

听了他的故事,我们很受感动。

We were all moved after we listened to his story.

他考得很好,受到了老师的表扬。

He got a good mark and was praised by his teacher.

这种新产品很受大家欢迎。

This kind of new products is popular among people.

2. 在爱情上/在婚姻中　　*zài àiqíng shang / zài hūnyīn zhōng*

"在……上"表示范围、方面或条件;"在……中"表示过程;以前还学过的"在……下"表示条件。这些小句一般做状语。例如:

"Zài……shang" indicates the scope, aspect or condition; "zài……zhōng" indicates the process and "zài……xià" indicates the condition. Generally these clauses act as adverbial modifier. For example:

我不想在考试上花那么多时间去准备。

I didn't want to spend too much time on the preparation of the examination.

Lesson Four The Chinese people's notion of love and marriage

在考试中他很紧张。

He was very nervous during the examination.

在这个问题上我们不要浪费太多的时间。

We shouldn't waste too much time discussing this problem.

在学习中可以不断地丰富我们自己。

We can enrich ourselves in the course of learning.

 Exercises

一 根据课文完成词语搭配 Complete the following word-collocations according to the text.

传统(　　　)　　　(　　　)的影响　　　(　　　)率

(　　　)的情况　　　纯洁的(　　　)　　　(　　　)的情感

二 选择填空 Choose the correct answers.

1. 我们的计划不会(　　)天气的影响。

   A 有　　　B 被　　　C 受　　　D 在

2. 这个法国姑娘(　　　)那个中国小伙子。

   A 结婚了　　B 嫁给了　　C 结婚给　　D 结婚和

3. 现代的年轻人在婚姻(　　)有了新的价值观念。

   A 下　　　B 上　　　C 中　　　D 里

4. 在帮助别人的过程(　　)我们自己也会找到快乐。

   A 下　　　B 上　　　C 中　　　D 内

SUCHENGZHONGWEN　47　速成中文

5. 这种办法的成功率很(　　)。
　　A 低　　　　B 好　　　　C 少　　　　D 多
6. 他对她表达爱情的方式真(　　)!
　　A 纯洁　　　B 开玩笑　　C 平等　　　D 浪漫

 模仿句型造句　Make sentences with the given words and sentence patterns.

1. 受……影响
2. ……之一
3. ……表现……

相关阅读
Related Reading

(一)

Zhēnghūn Qǐshì
征 婚 启 事

Nǚ, yījiǔqījiǔ nián qīyuè chūshēng, wèi hūn, shēngāo yī mǐ qīlíng,
女，1979 年 7 月 出生，未 婚，身 高 1 米 70，
dàzhuān, yòu'ér jiàoshī. Píngjūn yuè shōurù yìqiān~liǎngqiān yuán
大 专，幼 儿 教 师。 平 均 月 收 入 1000~2000 元
rénmínbì, Sìchuān Chéngdū hùkǒu, xiànzài Chéngdū jūzhù.
人 民 币，四 川 成 都 户 口，现 在 成 都 居 住。
Xúnzhǎo chéngshú wěnzhòng, zérèngǎn qiáng, wú bù liáng àihào de
寻 找 成 熟 稳 重，责 任 感 强，无 不 良 爱 好 的
nánshì wéi zhōngshēn bànlǚ. Rúguǒ nǐ quèdìng kěyǐ gěi wǒ
男 士 为 终 身 伴 侣。 如 果 你 确 定 可 以 给 我
níngjìng、wēnxīn de jiātíng shēnghuó, qǐng liánxì wǒ. Wǒ
宁 静、温 馨 的 家 庭 生 活，请 联 系 我。 我

Lesson Four The Chinese people's notion of love and marriage

jùjué yóuxì! Wúliáo wúguān wúsuǒwèi rénshì qǐng bú yào
拒绝 游戏！无聊 无关 无所谓 人士 请 不 要
dǎrǎo! Zhēnghūn dìqū: méiyǒu xiànzhì.
打扰！征婚 地区：没有 限制。

根据阅读内容判断正误：

1. 这个姑娘喜欢四川小伙子。　　　　　　　　（　）
2. 这个征婚的姑娘对男方的收入没有具体要求。（　）
3. 姑娘没有介绍自己的性格和爱好。　　　　　（　）

（二）

Mǒu jìzhě zài mǒu gāoxiào xuānchuánlán nèi jiàndào shù
某 记者 在 某 高校 宣传栏 内 见到 数
zhāng zhēnghūn qǐshì, shàngmian chēng, yí wèi zài mǒu gāoxiào rènjiào
张 征婚 启事，上面 称，一 位 在 某 高校 任教
de èrshíjiǔ suì wèihūn nǚ bóshì, "xiàngmào jiāohǎo, shēngāo
的 29 岁 未婚 女 博士，"相貌 姣好，身高
yī diǎn wǔbā mǐ, chuántǒng、tǐtiē, xiánshū, sùzhì gāo. Yù mì
1.58 米，传统、体贴、贤淑，素质高。欲 觅
shuòshì yǐshàng xuélì, sānshí'èr zhōusuì yǐxià, zài gāoxiào huò
硕士 以上 学历，32 周岁 以下，在 高校 或
jīguān shìyè dānwèi gōngzuò de nánshì wéi bàn".
机关 事业 单位 工作 的 男士 为 伴"。
Qǐshì shang hái fù yǒu xiángxì de liánxì diànhuà.
启事 上 还 附 有 详细 的 联系 电话。
Jìzhě ànzhào qǐshì shang liú de diànhuà hàomǎ dǎle
记者 按照 启事 上 留 的 电话 号码 打了

Chinese Crash Course

过去，接电话的人自称是女博士的姐姐。据她称，她和妹妹均是外地人，来济南刚刚一年，人地生疏，社交面窄。眼看妹妹的年龄越来越大，为了帮妹妹找到意中人，她就想出了在高校中张贴征婚启事的办法。当记者询问为何不通过婚介所或者媒体来征婚时，这位女士解释说，她感觉那样缺乏针对性，因为妹妹想找的理想对象应该是在高校或机关事业单位工作的男士，所以感觉在高校贴传单更直接，而且比较让人放心。

根据阅读内容判断正误：

1. 女博士是一名大学教师。　　　　　　　　　　（　）
2. 女博士找不到男友主要是因为社交面太窄。　　（　）
3. 女博士的男友最好是大学老师或公务员。　　　（　）

第5课 中国人的地方性格
Lesson Five The regional characters of the Chinese people

上海人小气，北京人懒惰，西北人老实，东北人野蛮，湖北人狡猾，浙江人太聪明……其实这都是片面的说法，你可千万别相信。

不过每个地方的人还是有自己的"地方性格"的。比如广东人喜欢做生意，又能吃苦，而北京人喜欢谈政治，最爱国；东北人讲究义气，看重朋友的感情；湖北人做事小心，但是不怕失败；上海人是好公民，爱整洁而且遵守法律；四川人聪明能干而又喜欢

Chinese Crash Course

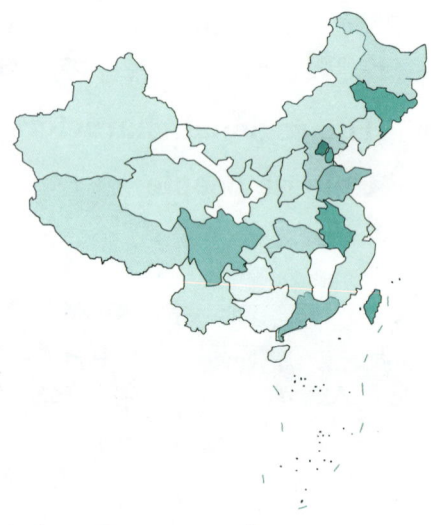

xiǎngshòu shēnghuó, Sìchuān nǚrén xiàng làjiāo yíyàng,
享受生活，四川女人像辣椒一样，
piàoliang ér lìhai; Xīběirén chéngshí, érqiě zài guānjiàn
漂亮而厉害；西北人诚实，而且在关键
de shíhou hěn yǒnggǎn; Zhèjiāngrén wēnhé, jiǎngjiu lǐmào,
的时候很勇敢；浙江人温和，讲究礼貌，
xiàng tāmen jiāxiāng de fēngjǐng yíyàng, xíngwéi gāoyǎ;
像他们家乡的风景一样，行为高雅；
Ānhuīrén àihào wénhuà, zhòngshì zhīshi, érqiě xǐhuan
安徽人爱好文化，重视知识，而且喜欢
zài wénhuà fāngmiàn tóuzī; Shānxīrén qínláo néng chīkǔ,
在文化方面投资；山西人勤劳能吃苦，
bǎ xìnyòng kànzuò shì zuì zhòngyào de.
把信用看做是最重要的。

　　Dāngrán hái yǒu hěn duō dìfang de rén, wǒmen shì
　　当然还有很多地方的人，我们是

Lesson Five　The regional characters of the Chinese people

shuō bu wán de. Zhōngguórén shuō zhè shì "yì fāng shuǐtǔ yǎng
说　不　完　的。中　国　人　说　这　是　"一　方　水　土　养
yì fāng rén", kànkan nǐ jiēchù de Zhōngguó péngyou, tāmen
一　方　人",看看　你　接　触　的　中　国　朋友，他们
shì shénme xìnggé de rén ne?
是　什么　性　格　的　人　呢?

　　People from Shanghai are stingy. People from Beijing are lazy. People from northwest are honest. People from northeast are wild. People from Hubei are cunning. People from Zhejiang are too smart. etc. As a matter of fact, these sayings are all one-sided. Never believe them.

　　Howerver, people from different regions do have their regional characters. For example, Cantonese like to do business and are able to bear hardships. People of Beijing like to talk about politics and they are the most patriotic. People from northeast are loyal to their friends. People from Hubei are careful and don't fear failure. Shanghainese are good citizens. They are interested in tidy and clean habits and obey the law. People from Sichuan are bright and capable, and like to enjoy life. The women of Sichuan are beautiful and bold, just like hot peppers. People from northwest are honest, and they are brave at the decisive moment. People from Zheijiang are sweet-tempered and they pay attention to manners. Their behaviours are as elegant as the scenery in Zhejiang. People from Anhui are fond of culture, and give importance to knowledge and they like to invest in culture industry. People from Shanxi are industrious, and they take credit as the most important thing.

There are also people from many other places that we can't talk them all. As a Chinese saying goes, "The water and land of one place foster the people of that place". Observe your Chinese friends that you are in contact with, what characters do they have?

生词 New Words

1.	小气	xiǎoqi	（形）	stingy
2.	懒惰	lǎnduò	（形）	lazy
3.	老实	lǎoshi	（形）	honest
4.	野蛮	yěmán	（形）	wild
5.	狡猾	jiǎohuá	（形）	cunning
6.	其实	qíshí	（副）	as a matter of fact
7.	片面	piànmiàn	（形）	one-sided
8.	说法	shuōfa	（名）	saying
9.	生意	shēngyi	（名）	business
10.	吃苦	chī//kǔ	（动）	bear hardships
11.	爱国	ài//guó	（动）	love one's country

Lesson Five　The regional characters of the Chinese people

12. 讲究	jiǎngjiu	（动、形）	pay attention to; tastful
13. 义气	yìqi	（名、形）	personal loyalty; chivalrous
14. 小心	xiǎoxīn	（动、形）	be careful; careful
15. 怕	pà	（动）	fear
16. 失败	shībài	（动）	fail
17. 公民	gōngmín	（名）	citizen
18. 整洁	zhěngjié	（形）	tidy
19. 遵守	zūnshǒu	（动）	obey
20. 能干	nénggàn	（形）	capable, competent
21. 辣椒	làjiāo	（名）	pepper
22. 厉害	lìhai	（形）	stern
23. 诚实	chéngshí	（形）	honest
24. 关键	guānjiàn	（形、名）	crucial; key
25. 温和	wēnhé	（形）	gentle
26. 礼貌	lǐmào	（名、形）	civility; polite
27. 风景	fēngjǐng	（名）	scenery
28. 高雅	gāoyǎ	（形）	elegant
29. 知识	zhīshi	（名）	knowledge
30. 勤劳	qínláo	（形）	industrious
31. 信用	xìnyòng	（名）	credit

Chinese Crash Course

 **专有名词　Proper Nouns**

1. 西北　　　Xīběi　　　　Northwest
2. 东北　　　Dōngběi　　　Northeast
3. 湖北　　　Húběi　　　　Hubei (Province)
4. 浙江　　　Zhèjiāng　　　Zhejiang (Province)
5. 广东　　　Guǎngdōng　　Guangdong (Province)
6. 安徽　　　Ānhuī　　　　Anhui (Province)
7. 山西　　　Shānxī　　　　Shanxi (Province)

 **句　型　Sentence Patterns**

1. 其实……

其实这是片面的说法。

As a matter of fact it was one-sided saying.

他们结婚五年了,其实她并不爱她的丈夫。

They have been married for five years but as a matter of fact she doesn't love her husband.

Lesson Five The regional characters of the Chinese people

2. 千万……

    你可千万别相信。

    Never believe them.

    明天你千万要来。

    Do come tomorrow.

3. ……,而……

    广东人喜欢做生意,又能吃苦,而北京人喜欢谈政治。

    Cantonese like to do business and are able to bear hardships, while Beijingers like to talk about politics.

    哥哥性格开朗,而弟弟却比较内向。

    The elder brother is outgoing, while the younger brother is a bit introverted.

4. 像……一样

    四川女人像辣椒一样,漂亮而厉害。

    The women of Sichuan are beautiful and bold, just like hot peppers.

    那是一个像天堂一样美丽的地方。

    That is a heavenly place.

5. 把……看做

    山西人把信用看做是最重要的。

    People from Shanxi take credit as the most important thing.

    我一直把她看做我的亲人。

    I take her as my family member all along.

 注 释　**Annotations**

1. 其实这是片面的说法　qíshí zhè shì piànmiàn de shuōfa

"其实"是副词,表示真实的情况或对上文的修正与补充。例如：

"Qíshí" is an adverb. It indicates the actual situation or corrects and complements what is mentioned earlier. For example:

他说话的口音像南方人,其实他是北方人。

His accent is like the southerner, but in fact he is a northerner.

她说自己是35岁,其实她38岁了。

She said that she is 35 years old, but as a matter of fact she is 38 years old.

书上说这段距离是30公里,其实只有20公里。

The book says that the distance is 30 kilometers, but actually it is only 20 kilometers.

2. 而　　ér

连词"而"可以连接并列的形容词或形容词性短语,表示相互补充。例如：

The conjunction "ér" can connect coordinate adjectives or adjective phrases which complement each other in meaning. For example:

四川人聪明能干而又喜欢享受生活。

People from Sichuan are bright and capable, and like to enjoy the life.

她美丽而善良。

She is both beautiful and kind.

Lesson Five The regional characters of the Chinese people

他是一位严肃而认真的老师。

He is a serious and earnest teacher.

"而"也可以表示转折,意为"但是、却。"例如:

"Ér" can also indicate the transition meaning "however or but". For example:

我们很有信心,而结果让我们很失望。

We were confident, but the result made us very disappointed.

北方还是大雪纷飞,而南方已经是春暖花开。

It's still snowy in the North, while it's already the warm spring with flowers in bloom in the South.

 Exercises

一 根据课文完成词语搭配 Complete the following word-collocations according to the text.

(　　)的说法	谈(　　)	讲究(　　)
看重(　　)	不怕(　　)	享受(　　)
关键的(　　)	行为(　　)	爱好(　　)
重视(　　)	接触(　　)	

二 选择填空　Choose the correct answers.

1. 他的理想是当一名教师,(　　)生活让他成为了一名军人。
   A 还有　　　B 而且　　　C 而　　　D 却

2. 广东人喜欢做生意,(　　)能吃苦。
   A 还有　　　B 不但　　　C 再　　　D 又

3. 做生意的人很(　　)信用。
   A 重要　　　B 看重　　　C 关键　　　D 看做

三 模仿句型造句　Make sentences with the given words and sentence patterns.

1. ……,而……

2. 其实……

3. 把……看做……

四 熟读下列描写人物性格特点的词语　Read the following words which describe human characters.

小气　懒惰　老实　勇敢　野蛮　聪明
狡猾　义气　小心　厉害　诚实　勤劳
温和　能吃苦

Lesson Five The regional characters of the Chinese people

相关阅读

Related Reading

（一）

头一回坐飞机去深圳，邻座是一位深圳女士。我们聊得很多，告别时我随口说了一句，希望以后有机会合作。女士马上打断我："这是你们北京的风格，我们深圳不是等有了机会再合作，而是坐在一起讨论合作的机会。这样吧，下了飞机我请你喝茶。"

有句名言："把一小时看做60分钟的人比别人的时间多60倍。"很显然，把每一个坐在对面的人都看做是一次机会的商人，肯定比有了机会再去把握的商人多100倍的机会。当时我就对深圳的商业文化及那位深圳

Chinese Crash Course

nǚshì fēicháng pèifu
女士非常佩服。

根据阅读内容判断正误：

1. 深圳女士喜欢喝茶。 （ ）
2. 深圳人喜欢抓住每一个经商合作的机会。 （ ）
3. 这个北京男人爱上了那位深圳女士。 （ ）

（二）

Dìlǐ tèzhēng duì rén de xìnggé yǒu hěn dà
地理特征对人的性格有很大
yǐngxiǎng. Wǒmen dōu zhīdao "hǎiyáng wénhuà" "huángtǔ
影响。我们都知道"海洋文化""黄土
wénhuà" zhè liǎng ge míngcí. Shānxī jiù shì huángtǔ
文化"这两个名词。山西就是黄土
wénhuà de dàibiǎo zhī yī. Shānxī yuǎn lí hǎiyáng, línjìn
文化的代表之一。山西远离海洋，临近
Huáng Hé, hǎiyáng de kāifàng wénhuà duì Shānxīrén de yǐngxiǎng
黄河，海洋的开放文化对山西人的影响
wēi hū qí wēi, ér shòu huángtǔ wénhuà hé Zhōngguó chuántǒng
微乎其微，而受黄土文化和中国传统
sīxiǎng de yǐngxiǎng, Shānxīrén jùyǒu hānhòu
思想的影响，山西人具有憨厚
pǔshí、xiāngduì shǒujiù de xìnggé tèdiǎn. Guǎngdōng zé shì
朴实、相对守旧的性格特点。广东则是
hǎiyáng wénhuà de dàibiǎo dìqū. Hǎiyáng wénhuà shì
海洋文化的代表地区。海洋文化是
kāifàng de wénhuà. Zài línjìn hǎiyáng de dìqū
开放的文化。在临近海洋的地区

Lesson Five　The regional characters of the Chinese people

shēnghuó, yǔ qítā guójiā hé dìqū hǎishàng hángxíng
生活，与其他国家和地区海上航行
jiāoliú de jīhuì hěn duō, shòu wàilái wénhuà de yǐngxiǎng
交流的机会很多，受外来文化的影响
yě duō. Zhèyàng jiù xíngchéngle Guǎngdōngrén bāoróng de
也多。这样就形成了广东人包容的
xīnlǐ tèzhēng, tāmen róngyì jiēshòu wàilái wénhuà hé
心理特征，他们容易接受外来文化和
xīnxiān shìwù.
新鲜事物。

　　Shāndōng de dìlǐ wèizhì bǐjiào tèshū, tā yì biān
　　山东的地理位置比较特殊，它一边
shēnxiàng Tàipíng Yáng, lìng yì biān shēnxiàng Huáng Hé, shòu hǎiyáng
伸向太平洋，另一边伸向黄河，受海洋
wénhuà hé huángtǔ wénhuà de shuāngchóng yǐngxiǎng; tóng-
文化和黄土文化的双重影响；同
shí tā chǔyú nánfāng hé běifāng de guòdù dìdài,
时它处于南方和北方的过渡地带，
suǒyǐ Shāndōngrén jùyǒu nánfāngrén hé běifāngrén
所以山东人具有南方人和北方人
de shuāngchóng xìnggé tèdiǎn: yì fāngmiàn jīngmíng nénggàn,
的双重性格特点：一方面精明能干，
lìng yì fāngmiàn háoshuǎng chōngdòng.
另一方面豪爽冲动。

根据阅读内容判断正误：
1. 山东人的性格有南方和北方综合在一起的特点。　　（　　）
2. 地理特征对人的性格确实有很大的影响。　　　　（　　）
3. 黄河文化区的人们性格大多保守。　　　　　　　（　　）

Dì Liù Kè Guānyú Jīngjù
第 6 课 关于京剧
Lesson Six About the Beijing opera

Zhōngguó de xìqǔ yìshù zhǒnglèi fēngfù, jīngjù
中国的戏曲艺术种类丰富，京剧
shì liúxíng zuì guǎng、yǐngxiǎng zuì dà、biǎoyǎn zuì chéngshú
是流行最广、影响最大、表演最成熟
de yì zhǒng. Jīngjù fánróngguo, yě chūxiànguo wēijī.
的一种。京剧繁荣过，也出现过危机。
Rújīn jīngjù yòu yǒule xīn de shēngmìnglì, hé xǔduō
如今京剧又有了新的生命力，和许多
chuántǒng yìshù yìqǐ dédàole jìchéng hé fāzhǎn.
传统艺术一起得到了继承和发展。

Lesson Six About the Beijing opera

京剧表演中,演员的功夫好,观众要立刻鼓励并喊"好!"这种热情的氛围是京剧表演特有的,演员不能缺少戏迷(也叫"票友")的鼓励和支持。

优秀的民族艺术也是属于世界的。有一些外国人迷上了京剧,专门来中国学习京剧。2001年京剧在德国引起了关注,演出结束后观众鼓掌长达10分钟还不肯退场。其实在100多年前,很多国外的戏剧家就已经在关注和研究京剧了,但是京剧的唱词太难翻译。希望有一天,外国人喜欢京剧不只是欣赏她鲜艳的服装和脸谱,而是能欣赏她的真正魅力。

The traditional Chinese operas are rich in variety. Beijing opera is the most popular one with enormous influence and great maturiy. It has flourished before and also had crises. Now it is full of vitality and is inherited and developed like the other traditional arts.

During a performance of the Beijing opera, when the actor or actress gave a brilliant display, the audience will shout out "good" to encourage him or her at once. This kind of exciting atmosphere is unique in Beijing opera's performing. Actors cannot lose the fans' support and encouragement.

The excellent national art also belongs to the world. Some foreigners also become fans of Beijing opera. They came to China on purpose to learn it. Beijing opera received great attention in Germany in 2001. At the end of the performance the audiences' applause lasted for 10 minutes and they weren't willing to leave. In fact, more than 100 years ago many foreign experts of dramas had already paid attention to Beijing opera and studied it. The translation of the librettos in Beijing opera is too difficult. The one and only hope is that foreigners not only enjoy the bright-colored costume and facial makeup but also the real charm of Beijing opera.

Lesson Six About the Beijing opera

 生　词　New Words

1. 戏曲艺术	xìqǔ yìshù		drama
2. 种类	zhǒnglèi	（名）	kind
3. 成熟	chéngshú	（形）	mature
4. 繁荣	fánróng	（形、动）	prosperous; flourish
5. 危机	wēijī	（名）	crisis
6. 如今	rújīn	（名）	now
7. 生命力	shēngmìnglì	（名）	vitality
8. 许多	xǔduō	（形）	many
9. 得到	dédào	（动）	get
10. 继承	jìchéng	（动）	inherit
11. 观众	guānzhòng	（名）	audience
12. 立刻	lìkè	（副）	immediately
13. 鼓励	gǔlì	（动）	encourage
14. 喊	hǎn	（动）	shout
15. 热情	rèqíng	（形）	enthusiastic
16. 氛围	fēnwéi	（名）	atmosphere
17. 特有	tè yǒu		unique
18. 缺少	quēshǎo	（动）	lack
19. 戏迷	xìmí	（名）	theatre fan

20. 票友	piàoyǒu	（名）	amateur performer
21. 民族	mínzú	（名）	nation, ethnic group
22. 专门	zhuānmén	（形）	special
23. 引起	yǐnqǐ	（动）	aroud
24. 关注	guānzhù	（动）	pay close attention
25. 鼓掌	gǔ//zhǎng	（动）	applaud
26. 肯	kěn	（动）	be willing to
27. 退场	tuì//chǎng	（动）	leave
28. 戏剧家	xìjùjiā	（名）	dramatist
戏剧	xìjù	（名）	drama, theater
29. 唱词	chàngcí	（名）	libretto
30. 欣赏	xīnshǎng	（动）	enjoy
31. 鲜艳	xiānyàn	（形）	bright-colored
32. 脸谱	liǎnpǔ	（名）	facial makeup
33. 真正	zhēnzhèng	（形、副）	real; really

 **Sentence Patterns**

1. ……，如今……

京剧出现过危机，如今又有了新的生命力。

Beijing opera once had crises. Now it is full of vitality again.

Lesson Six About the Beijing opera

这里以前是一片工业区,如今变成了美丽的花园小区。

Here was an industrial zone before and now it has become a beautiful garden housing estate.

2. 得到……

京剧得到了继承和发展。

Beijing opera gets inherited and developed.

这个项目得到了政府的关注和支持。

This project gets attention and support from the government.

3. 立刻……

演员的功夫好,观众要立刻鼓励并喊"好!"

When the actor gives an excellent performance, the audience will shout out "good!"

他看了我一眼,我立刻明白了他的意思。

He glanced at me and then I understood what he meant immediately.

4. 引起

2001年,京剧在德国引起了关注。

Beijing opera received great attention in Germany in 2001.

一个小小的错误也可能引起巨大的事故。

A little mistake may cause a big accident.

5. ……达

观众鼓掌长达十分钟还不肯退场。

The audience's applause lasted for 10 minutes and they weren't willing to leave.

这场明星演唱会的门票售价高达一千多元一张。

The admission ticket to the star concert has reached more than one thousand yuan.

6. 不只是……，而是……

希望有一天，外国人喜欢京剧不只是欣赏她鲜艳的服装和脸谱，而是能欣赏她的真正魅力。

The one and only hope is that foreigners not only enjoy the bright-colored costume and facial makeup but also the real charm of Beijing opera.

我喜欢她，不只是因为她的外表，而是还因为她有一颗纯洁的心。

I like her because she has not only an attractive appearance but also a pure heart.

注 释　Annotations

1. 迷上京剧 *míshang jīngjù*

这里的"上"在动词后做结果补语，表示达到了一定的程度、目的或标准。例如：

"Shàng" here acts as a complement of result indicating degree,

Lesson Six About the Beijing opera

purpose or standard. For example:

我喜欢上了北京。

I fell in love with Beijing.

我已经深深地爱上了这个姑娘。

I have fallen in love deeply with this girl.

他们已经买上了自己的房子。

They have already bought their own house.

2. 长达十分钟   cháng dá shí fēnzhōng

"达"后面接数量词,表示强调这个数量是到一定程度的。例如:

"Dá" is followed by a numeral-classifier compound to indicate that this amount has reached a rather high degree. For example:

这个大西瓜重达10公斤。

This big watermelon's weight has reached 10 kilograms.

这个建筑高达255米。

This building's height has reached 255 meters.

来参观的人每天多达一千人。

The number of visitors has reached one thousand each day.

3. 不仅……,而且……   bùjǐn……, érqiě……

这是表示递进关系的复句。"不仅"与"不但"用法相同,后面常跟"是",也可以说"不仅仅"。例如:

This is a progressive compound sentence. The usages of "bùjǐn" and "búdàn" are the same. They are usually followed by "shì". "Bùjǐnjǐn" is the same as "bùjǐn". For example:

这不仅是你一个人的事,也是我们大家的事。

This is not only your own business, but also ours.

我们不仅要学习汉语,而且还要多了解一些中国文化。

We not only have to learn Chinese, but also know some Chinese culture.

练习 Exercise

一 根据课文完成词语搭配 Complete the following word-collocations according to the text.

种类( )　　戏曲( )　　( )的生命力

传统( )　　继承( )　　( )的氛围

缺少( )　　优秀的( )　　引起( )

迷上( )　　欣赏( )　　鲜艳的( )

二 选择填空 Choose the correct answers.

1. 京剧繁荣( ),也出现过危机。
   A 了　　B 着　　C 吗　　D 过

2. 很多传统艺术( )了继承和发展。
   A 得　　B 被　　C 得到　　D 得上

3. 这个项目不能( )政府的支持。
   A 缺点　　B 缺少　　C 被　　D 引起

4. 我现在喜欢( )了中国的京剧。
   A 到　　B 过　　C 上　　D 着

Lesson Six About the Beijing opera

5. 这辆新车的价格高( )9万美元。

   A 了   B 有   C 多   D 达

 三 模仿句型造句 Make sentences with the given words and sentence patterns.

1. 得到……

2. 引起……

3. 不只是……，而是……

相关阅读
Related Reading

(一)

Jīngjù zuì dà de tèdiǎn huò mìmi jiù shì xūnǐ
京剧 最 大 的 特点 或 秘密 就 是 虚拟

xiěyì, jīngjù tóng Xīfāng huàjù de zuì dà qūbié jiù
写意，京剧 同 西 方 话剧 的 最 大 区别 就

zài zhèlǐ. Zài jīngjù de wǔtái shang, shíjiān hé kōngjiān
在 这里。 在 京剧 的 舞台 上， 时间 和 空间

shì zìyóu de, línghuó de. Yǎnyuán shuō "chūn nuǎn huā
是 自由 的， 灵活 的。 演员 说 "春 暖 花

kāi", guānzhòng jiù zhīdao shíjiān hé huánjìng le; kāi
开"， 观众 就 知道 时间 和 环境 了； 开

门、上楼、划船和骑马也是只用动作表现就可以；演员表演哭、喝酒也不用真那么做，而用写意的方法象征性地表演，这样的距离保持了戏曲的美感。《三岔口》中两个英雄在明亮的舞台上互相寻找，用来表示在黑夜里打斗，我们都是可以理解的，这就是京剧的虚拟性。

根据阅读内容判断正误：

1. 京剧的最大特点是夸张。（　　）
2. 京剧演员必须学会骑马和划船。（　　）
3. 京剧的表演同真实的生活相比是有一定距离的。（　　）

（二）

京剧是一门实践性很强的表演艺术。对青年演员来说，登台表演，积累舞台

Lesson Six　About the Beijing opera

经验尤其重要。在这次全国大赛的舞台上，京剧界的新秀们展示出来的技艺水平在评委眼中并不流俗。因此，对于所谓京剧人才一拨儿不如一拨儿的说法，于魁智认为这是对京剧演员不了解而产生的片面观点。

"大多数人并不了解现在的京剧演员，尤其是这些孩子们的想法与艺术追求。这次比赛中获奖的武生李阳名和武旦潘月娇两个孩子每天早晨七点钟就去练功房了，练得很刻苦。如果没有对艺术的追求与恒心，在舞台上是不可能有如此出色的表演的。"

采访中，于魁智也提出了本次大赛

中看到的些许担忧:京剧流派不够丰富。
"流派缺失,尤其是花脸组和老生组,花脸组只有两个派别,老生组和昔日的流派纷呈相比也单调了很多。如今,京剧的传承有待向更广的方面去拓展。"

根据阅读内容判断正误:

1. 现在,青年京剧演员的水平普遍下降。　　（　）
2. 京剧流派正在减少。　　　　　　　　　　（　）
3. 获奖的李阳名是唱武旦的。　　　　　　　（　）

第 7 课 海外华人
Lesson Seven Overseas Chinese

如果说中国是一棵大树，那么华人的历史就是树根的一部分。目前华人的准确数字很难统计，东南亚的华人最多，但是每个国家的情况不一样。前几年的资料表明，海外华人有6000万，他们的总资产达3万多亿美元。

为什么国外的华人大多来自福建和广东地区呢？从地理上看，福建和广东地区有海洋文化的特征，有向外发展的精神；从文化的角度解释，他们历史上就有经商的传统，8世纪的时候，这个地区就是经济发达地区，

Chinese Crash Course

南宋时泉州就是世界上最大的港口之一,意大利的马可·波罗在书中说"商人如云,货物如山",可以想象当时的经济是多么繁荣。华人在海外大多经商,也许正是受此影响。

海外华人成功的最大秘密就是勤劳、朴实、团结。他们形成了一个很强的文化圈子。现代社会的变化使华人控制的一些产业也有很多被改变了。但是印度尼西亚的华人圈子还有很强的实力,他们的产业是印尼经济最重要的部分。

从改革开放到现在,来自海外华人的投资也是中国经济发展的巨大力量。

Lesson Seven Overseas Chinese

If we say China is a big tree, the history of overseas Chinese is part of the tree root. The exact number of overseas Chinese is difficult to pin down at present. The number of overseas Chinese living in Southeast Asia is the largest, but the condition varies from country to country. Statistics of several years ago showed that there were 60 million overseas Chinese and their total assets have reached more than 3 trillion US dollars.

Why are overseas Chinese mostly from Fujian and Guangdong areas? Geographically, these two areas have the characteristic of marine culture and the pioneering spirit. Culturally, they had the tradition of doing business in their history. This area has been economically developed since the 8th century. Quanzhou in the Southern Song Dynasty was one of the biggest ports in the world. Marco Polo from Italy wrote that the businessmen came in large numbers and the goods were piled high like the hills. We can imagine how flourishing the economy of that time was! Most overseas Chinese doing business abroad was probably influenced by this culture.

The main secret of success of overseas Chinese is diligence, honesty and solidarity. They have formed a strong cultural circle. The changing of modern society has caused overseas Chinese to lose control of some industries. However,

Chinese Crash Course

the Chinese circle in Indonesia still has a strong strength and their industries cover the most important part of the Indonesian economy.

Since China's reform and opening up, the investment from overseas Chinese has been a huge strength of China's economic development.

 New Words

1.	华人	huárén	（名）	overseas Chinese
2.	棵	kē	（量）	*measure word*
3.	树	shù	（名）	tree
4.	树根	shùgēn	（名）	root of a tree
	根	gēn	（名）	root
5.	准确	zhǔnquè	（形）	exact
6.	数字	shùzì	（名）	number
7.	表明	biǎomíng	（动）	indicate
8.	资产	zīchǎn	（名）	property, assets
9.	亿	yì	（数）	a hundred million
10.	地理	dìlǐ	（名）	geography
11.	海洋	hǎiyáng	（名）	sea

Lesson Seven Overseas Chinese

12. 特征	tèzhēng	（名）		characteristic
13. 角度	jiǎodù	（名）		angle
14. 经商	jīng//shāng	（动）		do business
15. 世纪	shìjì	（名）		century
16. 发达	fādá	（形）		developed
17. 港口	gǎngkǒu	（名）		port
18. 云	yún	（名）		cloud
19. 山	shān	（名）		hill
20. 想象	xiǎngxiàng	（名、动）		imagination; imagine
21. 多么	duōme	（副）		how
22. 秘密	mìmì	（名）		secret
23. 朴实	pǔshí	（形）		plain
24. 团结	tuánjié	（动、形）		unite; united
25. 强	qiáng	（形）		strong
26. 圈子	quānzi	（名）		circle
27. 现代	xiàndài	（名、形）		modern times; modern
28. 控制	kòngzhì	（动）		control
29. 实力	shílì	（名）		strength
30. 巨大	jùdà	（形）		huge

专有名词 Proper Nouns

1.	东南亚	Dōngnányà	Southeast Asia
2.	福建	Fújiàn	Fujian (Province)
3.	南宋	Nánsòng	Southern Song Dynasty
4.	泉州	Quánzhōu	Quanzhou (City)
5.	意大利	Yìdàlì	Italy
6.	马可·波罗	Mǎkě·Bōluó	Marco Polo
7.	印度尼西亚	Yìndùníxīyà	Indonesia

句型 Sentence Patterns

1. 如果说……,那么……

如果说中国是一棵大树,那么华人的历史就是树根的一部分。

If we say China is a big tree, the history of overseas Chinese is part of the tree root.

如果说自由女神是美国的象征,那么万里长城就是中国的标志。

If we say the Statue of Liberty is the symbol of the United States, the Great Wall is the mark of China.

Lesson Seven Overseas Chinese

2. 表明……

前几年的统计数字表明,海外华人的数量是相当多的。

Statistics of several years ago indicated the number of overseas Chinese is quite large.

你的态度已经表明你是支持这个计划的。

Your attitude has indicated that you support this plan.

3. 总……

他们的总资产达3万多亿美元。

Their total assets have reached more than 3 trillion US dollars.

这家公司的总部在美国。

The headquarter of this company is located in the United States.

4. 为什么……呢?

为什么国外的华人大多来自福建和广东地区呢?

Why are overseas Chinese mostly from Fujian and Guangdong areas?

为什么这种现象在现代社会还在不断发生呢?

Why does this kind of phenomenon happen again and again in modern society?

5. 从……角度……

从文化的角度解释,他们历史上就有经商的传统。

Culturally, they had the tradition of doing business in their history.

从对外贸易发展的角度看,这个问题不会影响我们的合作。

From the perspective of developing foreign trade, this problem won't affect our cooperation.

6. 想象……

"商人如云,货物如山",可以想象当时的经济是多么繁荣!

"The businessmen came in large numbers and the goods were piled high like the hills." We can imagine how flourishing the economy of that time was!

我们不难想象他当时有多么兴奋。

We can imagine that how excited he was at that moment.

7. ……是……的部分

他们的产业是印尼经济最重要的部分。

Their industries cover the most important part of the Indonesia economy.

游戏产业现在也是IT产业的重要组成部分。

The game industry is an important part of IT industry now.

注 释 Annotations

1. 如果说……,那么……　　*Rúguǒ shuō……, nàme……*

在这个复句中,两个句子之间有类比的意思,不是简单的假设或条件复句。例如:

The two clauses in this compound sentence form an analogy. From example:

如果说价值观念是企业发展的重要部分,那么鼓励员工成为企业的

Lesson Seven　Overseas Chinese

"英雄"就是合理的。

If we say the values are the important part of enterprises' development, then it is reasonable to encourage employees to become the "heroes" of enterprises.

如果说一次考试成绩不能说明能力,那么这么多次考试成绩不好还不能说明一个人的能力吗?

If the score of one exam can't prove one's ability, then can many poor scores prove it?

2. 从……的角度……　　*cóng……de jiǎodù……*

这个结构常做状语,用在分析或说理性的句子中,表示看问题的不同方面。例如:

This structure often acts as an adverbial in an analytic or reasoning sentence to indicate different aspects of a problem. For example:

从法律的角度看,这种行为是完全合理的;而从情感的角度看,一般人又是很难接受的。

From the legal point of view, this behavior is completely reasonable, while from the emotional perspective it can't be accepted by ordinary people.

从企业的角度看,这种做法是非常有效的;但是从政府的角度看,这就增加了管理的困难。

From the enterprises' perspective, this method is very effective. But the government thinks that it increases the difficulty of management.

练 习 Exercises

一、**根据课文完成词语搭配** Complete the following word-collocations according to the text.

准确的(　　)　　(　　)表明　　海外(　　)
(　　)文化　　向外(　　)　　经济(　　)
现代(　　)　　控制(　　)　　(　　)的实力
(　　)部分　　(　　)力量

二、**选择填空** Choose the correct answers.

1. 如果说祖国是一棵大树,(　　)我就是一片树叶。
　A 这么　　B 还有　　C 而且　　D 那么

2. 这些来(　　)美国的留学生对中国文化很感兴趣。
　A 从　　B 至　　C 了　　D 自

3. 从文化的(　　)看,这些建筑应该受到保护。
　A 方法　　B 角度　　C 表明　　D 圈子

4. 海外华人的投资是中国经济发展的巨大(　　)。
　A 部分　　B 力量　　C 影响　　D 控制

5. 你能(　　)20年以后我们的生活会是什么样子吗?
　A 控制　　B 觉得　　C 想象　　D 忘记

Lesson Seven Overseas Chinese

三 模仿句型造句　Make sentences with the given words and sentence patterns.

1. 如果说……,那么……

2. 从……的角度……

3. ……是……的部分

相关阅读
Related Reading

"Biàn bù quánqiú de huáshāng yìzhí shì tuīdòng Yà-Tài
"遍布全球的华商一直是推动亚太
dìqū jīngjì chéngzhǎng hé yìtǐhuà de qiáoliáng yǔ
地区经济成长和一体化的桥梁与
niǔdài. Běn jiè huáshāng dàhuì jiāng cùshǐ quánqiú
纽带。本届华商大会将促使全球
huárén qǐyè yǔ Hánguó qǐyè jiāqiáng jiāoliú,
华人企业与韩国企业加强交流,
kāituò xīn lǐngyù, xúnqiú xīn shāngjī." Hánguó guówù
开拓新领域,寻求新商机。"韩国国务
zǒnglǐ Lǐ Hǎizàn rúcǐ biǎoshì. Zài huáshāng rénshù
总理李海瓒如此表示。在华商人数

相对较少、影响相对较弱的韩国,政府已开始重视华商巨大的经济能量,并投入很大力量主办本届世界华商大会,希望通过加强与全球华商的交流与合作,扩大对外经贸交往,加速本国经济发展,实现"与华商共成长,与世界共繁荣"的大会宗旨。

韩国媒体十分关注本届世界华商大会。大会开幕前夕,已连续多日给予了大量报道。

据称,为期三天的大会将举办信息技术、生物技术、文化信息技术等多场专题研讨会及名人讲座;将举办华商投资和韩国投资说明会以及华商、韩商的CEO会议。大会还将组织

Lesson Seven Overseas Chinese

shìjiè huárén qǐyèjiā zài Hánguó jìnxíng chǎnyè yǔ
世界华人企业家在韩国进行产业与
wénhuà kǎochá. Dàhuì nèiróng bùjǐn fēngfù, érqiě wùshí.
文化考察。大会内容不仅丰富，而且务实。

根据阅读内容判断正误：

1. 华商在韩国的影响很大，而且数量较多。　　　（　）
2. 韩国政府开始重视同全球华人的合作。　　　　（　）
3. 韩国媒体表现很积极，起到了很好的作用。　　（　）

第8课 成语故事（一）
Lesson Eight　Idiom story (1)

一口井里住着一只青蛙。有一天，青蛙在井边碰到了一只从海里来的大海龟。

青蛙对海龟说："你看，我住在这里多快乐！有时高兴了，就在井边跳一跳；有时累了，就回到井里，安安静静地把全身泡在水里，或者在泥里散步，也很舒服。谁也比不上我。而且，我是这个井的主人，自由自在，你为什么不来呢？"

Lesson Eight Idiom story (1)

海龟听了青蛙的话,说:"你看过海吗?海是广大的,谁也不知道海的深度。即使世界上所有的河流都流向大海,海里的水也不会变多;即使十年不下雨,海里的水也不会变浅。住在大海里,才是真正的快乐呢!"

青蛙听了海龟的话,吃惊地蹲在那里,再也不说话了。

这就是"井底之蛙"的故事,比喻受环境的限制而没有知识、见识少、眼光短浅的人。例如,"他就是个井底之蛙,根本不知道外面的世界,你不要听他的意见"。

Once there was a frog that lived in a well. One day this frog met a marine turtle from the sea at the edge of the well. The frog said to the turtle, "Look, how happily I live here! When I am happy I can jump near the well; when I am tired I come back to the well and soak myself in water peacefully or take a leisurely walk in the mud. No one is as comfortable as me; I am the owner of the well and live freely. Why don't you come?"

After listening to the frog, the turtle said: "Have you ever seen the sea? It is immense and nobody knows how deep it is. All the rivers flow into the sea, its water won't become more. Even the drought lasts for ten years it won't dry. When living in the sea, you will have the real happiness."

After listening to the marine turtle's words, the frog squatted there in astonishment and said nothing.

This is the story of "a frog in a well". It is a metaphor for the people who lack knowledge and experience and are shortsighted because they are confined by the environment. For example, "He is a frog in a well and he doesn't know the outside world at all. Don't listen to his opinion."

Lesson Eight Idiom story (1)

 生 词 New Words

1.	井	jǐng	(名)	well
2.	只	zhī	(量)	*measure word*
3.	青蛙	qīngwā	(名)	frog
4.	碰	pèng	(动)	meet
5.	海龟	hǎiguī	(名)	sea turtle, marine turtle
6.	有时	yǒushí	(副)	sometimes
7.	跳	tiào	(动)	jump
8.	安静	ānjìng	(动、形)	quiet; noiseless
9.	泡	pào	(动)	soak
10.	泥	ní	(名)	mud
11.	散步	sàn//bù	(动)	take a walk
12.	主人	zhǔrén	(名)	owner
13.	自由自在	zìyóu zìzài		free
14.	广大	guǎngdà	(形)	immense
15.	深度	shēndù	(名)	depth
16.	即使	jíshǐ	(连)	even if
17.	河流	héliú	(名)	river
	河	hé	(名)	river
18.	流	liú	(动)	flow

Chinese Crash Course

19.	浅	qiǎn	(形)	shallow
20.	吃惊	chī//jīng	(动)	surprise
21.	蹲	dūn	(动)	squat
22.	井底之蛙	jǐng dǐ zhī wā		a frog in a well
23.	比喻	bǐyù	(名、动)	metaphor; liken to
24.	限制	xiànzhì	(动)	confine
25.	见识	jiànshi	(名)	insight
26.	眼光	yǎnguāng	(名)	vision
27.	短浅	duǎnqiǎn	(形)	shortsighted
28.	例如	lìrú	(动)	take for example
29.	根本	gēnběn	(名、副)	root; at all

 **Sentence Patterns**

1. 有时……,有时……

有时高兴了,就在井边跳一跳;有时累了,就回到井里。

When I am happy I can jump near the well, when I am tired I come back to the well.

他在书房已经待了5个小时了,有时低头看书,有时又像在思考问题。

He has been in his study for 5 hours. Sometimes he lowered his head to read, sometimes he seemed to be thinking.

Lesson Eight Idiom story (1)

2. 比不上/比得上

谁也比不上我。

Nobody can be compared with me.

我的汉语水平可比不上他。

My Chinese level is no match for him.

她跑得真快,比得上专业运动员了。

She runs so fast that she can match up to professional athletes.

3. 再不/没……了

青蛙听了海龟的话,再也不说话了。

The frog said nothing after listening to the marine turtle's words.

我再不去那个地方了,真没意思!

I will never go to that place again. It is extremely boring!

4. 根本……

他就是个井底之蛙,根本不知道外面的世界。

He is a frog in a well and he doesn't know the outside world at all.

谁也没告诉过我,我根本就不知道这件事。

No one told me that thing. I didn't know it at all.

Chinese Crash Course

注 释　Annotations

1. 安静——安安静静　　ānjìng—ānān-jìngjìng

有些AB式形容词可以变成AABB的重叠形式,表示程度的加深,多做状语或补语。例如:

Some adjectives of AB pattern can be reduplicated in the form of AABB, indicating the increase of degree. They usually act as adverbial or complement. For example:

他把房间打扫得干干净净的。

He cleaned the room neatly and tidily.

她打扮得漂漂亮亮的,准备去见男朋友。

She made herself up very beautifully and was going to meet her boyfriend.

我要快快乐乐地度过我的假期。

I will spend my holiday happily.

2. 即使　　jíshǐ

"即使"后面常用"也"呼应,"即使"表示一种假设情况,"也"后面表示结果或结论不受这种情况的影响。例如:

"Jíshǐ" is often echoed with "yě" in the latter half of a concessive compound sentence. The former half introduced by "jíshǐ" gives a supposition. "Yě" indicates that the conclusion or result will not be changed under such circumstances. For example:

即使成功的机会很小,我也会努力争取。

I will try hard though there is minimal chance to succeed.

Lesson Eight Idiom story (1)

即使世界上只有你一个男人,我也不会跟你结婚。
Even if there was only one man in the world, I wouldn't marry you.
即使你们都不同意,我也要那么做。
Even if you all don't agree, I will still do it.

3. 再不/没……了   zài bù / méi …… le

"再"或"再也"后接否定副词"不"或"没",表示不想、不会或没有再发生。例如:

"Zài" or "zài yě" is followed by negative adverb "bù" or "méi" to indicate that one doesn't want to or won't do something any more, or something won't happen anymore. For example:

这次如果失败了,你就再也没有机会了。
If you fail this time you will not have any chance at all.
我再不会做那样的错事了。
I will never make that kind of mistake again.
你再也不要给我打电话了,我讨厌你!
Don't call me any more. I hate you!

练 习 Exercises

一 根据课文完成词语搭配 Complete the following word-collcations according to the text.

广大的(　　)　　海的(　　)　　真正的(　　)
眼光(　　)　　吃惊地(　　)　　受(　　)的限制

Chinese Crash Course

二 选择填空 Choose the correct answers.

1. "井底之蛙"用来(　　)受环境限制而目光短浅的人。
　A 说明　　　B 比喻　　　C 表明　　　D 表现

2. 这个外国人的汉语水平真高,完全比(　　)中国人。
　A 不上　　　B 不了　　　C 上　　　　D 得上

3. 这场比赛(　　)胜利我都高兴,因为我不是任何一方的支持者。
　A 他们队　　B 你们队　　C 谁　　　　D 我们队

4. 我把(　　)的秘密都告诉你了。
　A 一切　　　B 全　　　　C 都　　　　D 所有

5. (　　)困难很多,我也要完成这个工作。
　A 因为　　　B 不但　　　C 即使　　　D 而且

6. 她走了,从此,(　　)没有她的消息了。
　A 在　　　　B 还　　　　C 所有　　　D 再

三 模仿句型造句 Make sentences with the given words and sentence patterns.

1. 比不上

2. 再不/没……了

3. 根本……

Lesson Eight Idiom story (1)

相关阅读
Related Reading

成语是汉语词汇中特有的一种长期使用的固定短语。成语一般来自于古代经典、著名作品或历史故事和人们的口头语言,它的意义常常隐含于字面意思之中,不是表面意义的简单相加,具有意义的整体性。它结构紧密,一般不能任意变动词序;形式以四字格居多,也有少量三字格和多字格的。

使用成语不仅可以说明问题,而且可以使你的汉语变得生动而丰富。多学一些成语,多说一些成语,你一定会发现更多学习汉语的乐趣。

Chinese Crash Course

根据阅读内容判断正误:

1. 一般中国人不喜欢用成语。　　　　　　　　(　)
2. 四字成语并不多。　　　　　　　　　　　　(　)
3. 成语大多来自古代经典或历史故事。　　　　(　)

第 9 课 成语故事（二）
Lesson Nine　Idiom story (2)

从前在杞国，有一个胆子很小的人。他常会想一些莫名其妙的问题，让人觉得很奇怪。

有一天，他自言自语地说："假如有一天，天塌了下来，我们没有地方躲藏，那么我们都会被压死。这可怎么办呢？"

从此以后，他几乎每天都在为这个问题发愁、烦恼，朋友见他精神不好，都为他担心。但是，当大家

Chinese Crash Course

zhīdao yuányīn hòu, jiù quàn tā shuō: "Nǐ hébì wèi zhè
知道原因后，就劝他说："你何必为这

jiàn shì fánnǎo ne? Tiānkōng zěnme huì tā xialai ne?
件事烦恼呢？天空怎么会塌下来呢？

Zàishuō, jíshǐ zhēn tā xialai, yě bú shì nǐ yí ge rén
再说，即使真塌下来，也不是你一个人

fāchóu jiù kěyǐ jiějué de a!"
发愁就可以解决的啊！"

Kěshì, wúlùn rénjia zěnme shuō, tā dōu bù
可是，无论人家怎么说，他都不

xiāngxìn, réngrán wèi zhège bú bìyào de wèntí dānyōu.
相信，仍然为这个不必要的问题担忧。

Hòulái de rén jiù gēnjù zhège gùshì,
后来的人就根据这个故事，

yǐnshēn chū "Qǐ rén yōu tiān" zhè jù chéngyǔ, tā zhǔyào
引申出"杞人忧天"这句成语，它主要

shì gàosu rénmen búyào wèi yìxiē bù shíjì de
是告诉人们不要为一些不实际的

shìqing ér yōuchóu. Lìrú: "Nǐ bié Qǐ rén yōu tiān le,
事情而忧愁。例如："你别杞人忧天了，

wàixīngrén shì bú huì lái dìqiú de; zhēn de lái le,
外星人是不会来地球的；真的来了，

yě bú huì lái zhǎo nǐ de."
也不会来找你的。"

Once upon a time, there was a coward in the state of Qi. He often thought about weird questions without rhyme or reason and this made other people feel strange.

One day, he spoke to himself, "If the sky collapses some

Lesson Nine Idiom story (2)

day and we have no place to hide then all of us would be pressed to death. What should we do?"

From then on, he was worried and troubled by this question nearly every day. His friends saw that his spirit wasn't high and they all worried about him. When people knew the reason, they console him: "Don't worry about that. How will the sky collapse? Even if it falls down you can't solve the problem by yourself."

But no matter how other people persuaded him he ignored it and still worried about the unnecessary problem.

Since then people got the idiom "like the man of Qi who was afraid of the sky falling" according to the above story. It mainly tells people: Don't worry about the unpractical matters. For example: Don't meet trouble half-way. The extraterrestrial being won't come to the earth. Even if they really come, they won't come to you.

生 词 New Words

1. 从前   cóngqián   (名)   once upon a time
2. 胆子   dǎnzi   (名)   courage
3. 莫名其妙 mò míng qí miào   without rhyme or reason

Chinese Crash Course

4. 奇怪	qíguài	（形）		strange
5. 自言自语	zì yán zì yǔ			speak to oneself
6. 假如	jiǎrú	（连）		if
7. 塌	tā	（动）		collapse
8. 躲藏	duǒcáng	（动）		hide
9. 压	yā	（动）		press
10. 几乎	jīhū	（副）		nearly
11. 发愁	fā//chóu	（动）		be anxious
12. 烦恼	fánnǎo	（形）		vexed
13. 原因	yuányīn	（名）		reason
14. 劝	quàn	（动）		persuade
15. 何必	hébì	（副）		there is no need
16. 天空	tiānkōng	（名）		sky
17. 再说	zàishuō	（连）		what is more
18. 无论	wúlùn	（连）		no matter what
19. 人家	rénjia	（代）		others
20. 仍然	réngrán	（副）		still
21. 必要	bìyào	（形）		necessary
22. 担忧	dānyōu	（动）		worry
23. 根据	gēnjù	（介）		according to
24. 引申	yǐnshēn	（动）		extend
25. 杞人忧天	Qǐ rén yōu tiān			like the man of Qi who feared that the sky might fall

Lesson Nine　Idiom story (2)

26. 实际	shíjì	（形、名）	practical; reality
27. 忧愁	yōuchóu	（形）	worried
28. 外星人	wàixīngrén	（名）	extraterrestrial being
29. 地球	dìqiú	（名）	earth

　**Sentence Patterns**

1. 几乎……

从此以后,他几乎每天都在为这个问题发愁。

From then on, he was worried and troubled by this question nearly every day.

这一年来他几乎天天去喝酒。

Almost everyday in this year he goes to drink.

2. ……,再说,……

天空怎么会塌下来呢？再说,即使真塌下来,也不是你一个人能解决的。

How will the sky collapse? Even if it really falls down, you can't solve the problem by yourself.

他的工作特别忙,再说,他最近的身体也不好,我真为他担心。

He is extremely busy with his work. And what's more, he is in the poor state of health recently. I really worry about him.

3. 无论……,都/也……

无论人家怎么说,他都不相信。

No matter how other people persuaded him, he ignored it.

无论什么人都不能不遵守法律。

Whoever should obey the law.

4. 仍然……

他不相信别人的说法,仍然为这个问题担忧。

He wouldn't believe others' saying. He was still worried about this problem.

她已经嫁给了别人,但他仍然深深地爱着她。

Although she was married to someone else, he was still loving her deeply.

5. 根据……

后来的人就根据这个故事,引申出"杞人忧天"这句成语。

Since then people got the idiom "like the man of Qi who was afraid of the sky falling" according to the above story.

根据我们的统计,这里的环境问题很严重。

The environmental problem here is very serious according to our statistics.

注 释 Annotations

1. 无论……,都/也……　　wúlùn……, dōu / yě……

连词"无论"表示在任何条件下结果或结论都不会改变,前句常有表

Lesson Nine Idiom story (2)

任指的疑问代词或表示选择的句子,后面常有"都"或"也"呼应。例如:

The conjunction "wúlùn" indicates that the result or conclusion won't change under any circumstances. The former clause always has an arbitrary interrogative pronoun or is an alternative sentence, and after it, it always has "dōu" or "yě" to echo with it. For example:

无论做什么工作,他都非常认真。

He is very earnest no matter what work he is engaged in.

无论是城市还是农村,到处都呈现出一片新景象。

No matter in the city or the countryside, everywhere is taking on a new look.

无论困难有多么大,我们都要坚持下去。

We should hold on no matter how great the difficulty is.

2. 为不实际的事情而忧愁   wèi bù shíjì de shìqing ér yōuchóu

这里的"而"表示先后承接或递进的关系,而不是转折或并列意义的连接。例如:

"Ér" here indicates a successive or progressive relationship. It dosen't indicate the succession of transition or coordination. For example:

他们为了事业的发展而努力地工作。

They work hard for their careers.

你们不要因为失败而放弃一切。

Don't give up everything because of failure.

 练 习 Exercises

一 选择成语填空 Fill in the blanks with the proper idioms.

莫名其妙　　　自言自语　　　杞人忧天

井底之蛙　　　自由自在

1. 他住在高楼里,天天担心高楼会塌下来,真是(　　　)!
2. 请你多出去见识一下再作决定,不要待在家里像个(　　　)。
3. 他一个人坐在那里(　　　),谁也不知道他在说什么。
4. 我喜欢(　　　)的生活,不喜欢受限制。
5. 她最近情绪不太正常,经常(　　　)地哭起来。

二 选择填空 Choose the correct answers.

1. 他常会问些莫名其妙的问题(　　),让我们觉得奇怪。

  A 再　　　B 而　　　C 而且　　　D 然而

2. (　　)我们说什么,他都不听。

  A 即使　　B 因为　　C 不但　　　D 无论

3. (　　)我们的调查,这种产品现在在市场上很受欢迎。

  A 根据　　B 因为　　C 无论　　　D 在

4. 你不要担心,(　　),那么多朋友都会帮助你的。

  A 再见　　B 再说　　C 但是　　　D 无论

Lesson Nine Idiom story (2)

三 模仿句型造句 Make sentences with the given words and sentence patterns.

1. ……,再说,……

2. 无论……,都/也……

3. 仍然

相关阅读
Related Reading

（一）

许多中国人爱用成语、俗语,但是按字面翻译成英语时,容易变成 Chinese English. 我们来看看下面几个正确的翻译。

1. 人山人海(rén shān rén hǎi)：在诗词用语 (poetic expression) 里,用 a (the) sea of faces.

2. 家家有本难念的经(Jiājiā yǒu běn nán niàn de jīng.)：Every family has its own problems.

Chinese Crash Course

3. 天下没有不散的筵席(Tiānxià méiyǒu bú sàn de yánxí.)：All good things must come to an end. 或 Eventually, all bosom friends will drift apart.

4. 平时不烧香，临时抱佛脚(Píngshí bù shāo xiāng, línshí bào fó jiǎo.)：Do nothing till one is driven to desperation.

5. 挂羊头，卖狗肉(guà yángtóu, mài gǒuròu)：Say one thing and do another.

6. 一言既出，驷马难追(yì yán jì chū, sì mǎ nán zhuī)：A word once let go cannot be recalled.

7. 祸从口出，言多必失(huò cóng kǒu chū, yán duō bì shī)：The less said the better.

（二）

Yóuyú Zhōng-Xīfāng de shèhuì wénhuà cúnzàizhe hěn
由于中西方的社会文化存在着很
dà de chāyì, qí yǔyán yě bìrán huì yǒu hěn dà de
大的差异，其语言也必然会有很大的
chābié. Yǔyán lí bu kāi wénhuà, wénhuà yě lí bu kāi
差别。语言离不开文化，文化也离不开
yǔyán. Xiàmiàn jiù Yīng Hàn shúyǔ duìyì de jǐ ge
语言。下面就英汉熟语对译的几个
shílì, lái kànkan liǎng zhǒng yǔyán zài shúyǔ zhōng suǒ
实例，来看看两种语言在熟语中所
tǐxiàn de wénhuà chāyì.
体现的文化差异。

Tā zhuàng de xiàng tóu niú.
(1) 他壮得像头牛 (ox)。
He is as strong as a horse (马).　　(牛 niú —— 马 mǎ)

Lesson Nine Idiom story (2)

(2) 她 胆 小 如 鼠 (mouse)。
　　Tā dǎn xiǎo rú shǔ.
　　She is as timid as a hare (兔).　　　　(鼠 shǔ —— 兔 tù)

(3) 养 虎 (tiger) 遗 患
　　yǎng hǔ   yí huàn
　　warm a snake (蛇) in one's bosom (虎 hǔ —— 蛇 shé)

(4) 瓮 中 之 鳖
　　wèng zhōng zhī biē
　　like a rat (鼠) in a hole　　　　(鳖 biē —— 鼠 shǔ)

(5) 害 群 之 马 (horse)
　　hài qún zhī mǎ
　　black sheep (羊)　　　　　　(马 mǎ —— 羊 yáng)

(6) 对 牛 (cow) 弹 琴
　　duì niú   tán qín
　　Cast pearls before swine (猪)　　(牛 niú —— 猪 zhū)

(7) 落 汤 鸡 (rooster) / 落 水 狗 (dog)
　　luò tāng jī   / luò shuǐ gǒu
　　like a drowned mouse (鼠)　(鸡/狗 jī/gǒu —— 鼠 shǔ)

(8) 热 锅 上 的 蚂 蚁 (ant)
　　rè guō shang de mǎyǐ
　　like a cat (猫) on hot bricks　(蚂蚁 mǎyǐ —— 猫 māo)

(9) 宁 为 鸡 (rooster) 头, 毋 为 牛 (ox) 后。
　　Nìng wéi jī   tóu, wú wéi niú   hòu.
　　Better be the head of a dog (狗) than the tail of a lion (狮).
　　　　　　　(鸡 jī —— 狗 gǒu, 牛 niú —— 狮 shī)

由 此 可 见, 汉 语 熟 语 中 的 表 示 某
Yóu cǐ kě jiàn, Hànyǔ shúyǔ zhōng de biǎoshì mǒu

Chinese Crash Course

yì xiàngzhēng yìyì de dòngwù hé Yīngyǔ yànyǔ zhōng
一象征意义的动物和英语谚语中
de dòngwù shì wánquán bù tóng de.
的动物是完全不同的。

第 10 课 一封情书
Lesson Ten　A love letter

亲爱的：

你好！知道我有多想你吗？每当想起你，我都会感到很幸福，但是你对我来说是那么遥远。我的宝贝，每次与你相见，都让我惊奇，惊奇你的美丽，你的温柔。

夜已很深了，窗外一直下着雨。我总算知道了古人说的"一日不见，如隔三秋"是种什么样的感觉了，真痛苦啊！

你会想到失去的可怕吗？你会想到珍惜眼前的一切吗？可是我一个人

怎么能把握住我们的幸福呢？我真诚地希望你能珍惜我们的一切。

爱上你以后，我才知道思念有多苦，我才体会到爱的甜蜜。谢谢你给我的爱。相信我，相信我的真心，我爱的就是你，永远是你！没有任何人可以代替你，你是我心中永远的、最可爱的天使！

我想看你的微笑，抚摸你的脸，听到你的声音，让我的梦中充满爱。

睡吧，我的宝贝，吻你！

深爱你的人
7月31日于家中

Lesson Ten A love letter

Darling,

How are you? Do you know how much I miss you? I feel very happy whenever I think of you, but you are so far away from me. My baby, you make me surprised each time I see you. I am surprised at your beauty and your tenderness.

It is very late and it is raining all along. I eventually know the meaning of what the ancients said: We didn't meet for one day but it is just like we have been separated for three years. This is killing me!

Will you think of a scare about loss? Will you think of treasuring everthing at present? How can I hold the happiness of ours by myself? I sincerely hope that you can treasure everthing we have.

I didn't know the bitterness of concern and the sweetness of love until I fell in love with you. Thank you for giving your love to me. Believe me and my sincerity. You are my only love and I will have everlasting love for you. No one can take the place of you and you are the loveliest angel in my heart.

I want to see your smile, touch your face and listen to your voice. You make my dreams full of love.

Sweet dream, my baby, kiss you.

The one who deeply loves you

31st, July

at home

Chinese Crash Course

生　词　New Words

1.	封	fēng	（量）	*measure word*
2.	情书	qíngshū	（名）	love letter
3.	亲爱的	qīn'ài de		darling
	亲爱	qīn'ài	（形）	dear
4.	遥远	yáoyuǎn	（形）	far
5.	宝贝	bǎobèi	（名）	baby
6.	惊奇	jīngqí	（动）	surprise
7.	温柔	wēnróu	（形）	gentle and soft
8.	总算	zǒngsuàn	（副）	eventually
9.	隔	gé	（动）	separate
10.	感觉	gǎnjué	（名、动）	feeling; feel
11.	痛苦	tòngkǔ	（形）	painful
12.	失去	shīqù	（动）	lose
13.	可怕	kěpà	（形）	fearful
14.	眼前	yǎnqián	（名）	at present
15.	把握	bǎwò	（动）	hold
16.	真诚	zhēnchéng	（形）	sincere
17.	思念	sīniàn	（动）	miss
18.	体会	tǐhuì	（动）	experience

Lesson Ten   A love letter

19. 真心	zhēnxīn	（名）	sincerity
心	xīn	（名）	heart
20. 永远	yǒngyuǎn	（副）	forever
21. 代替	dàitì	（动）	take the place of
22. 可爱	kě'ài	（形）	lovely
23. 天使	tiānshǐ	（名）	angel
24. 微笑	wēixiào	（动）	smile
25. 抚摸	fǔmō	（动）	touch
26. 脸	liǎn	（名）	face
27. 声音	shēngyīn	（名）	sound
28. 梦	mèng	（名）	dream
29. 充满	chōngmǎn	（动）	fill
30. 吻	wěn	（名、动）	kiss; kiss
31. 于	yú	（介）	at

 **Sentence Patterns**

1. 每当

每当想起你，我都会感到很幸福。

I feel very happy whenever I think of you.

每当回到故乡，我都会有一种平和的感觉。

I would have a feeling of peacefulness whenever I returned to my hometown.

Chinese Crash Course

2. 对……来说

但是你对我来说是那么遥远。

You are so far away from me.

考试对学生来说,并不是最重要的事情。

Examination is not the most important thing to the students.

3. 总算……

我总算知道古人说的话是什么意思了。

I eventually know the meaning of the ancients' words.

我总算等到他回来了。

I finally saw him back.

4. 才……

爱上你以后,我才体会到爱的甜蜜。

I didn't know the sweetness of love until I fell in love with you.

来到中国以后,我才有了学习汉语的快乐。

I didn't get a lot of pleasure of learning Chinese until I came to China.

5. 代替……

没有任何人可以代替你。

No one can take the place of you.

可以用这种药物代替那种药物。

This kind of medicine can take the place of that one.

Lesson Ten A love letter

注 释 Annotations

1. 对……来说 duì……lái shuō

"对……来说"用来引进涉及的对象,做状语。例如:

"Duì……lái shuō" is used for introducing the object involved and acts as an adverbial. For example:

失去父亲对一个15岁的孩子来说太痛苦了。

It is too painful for a child of fifteen years old to lose his father.

写汉字对欧美学生来说太难了,而对日本、韩国同学来说就容易多了。

Writing characters is too difficult for the students from Europe and America while it is much easier for Japanese and South Korean students.

会说两门外语对一个现代人来说不是很高的要求。

It is not a high requirement for a modern person to speak two foreign languages.

2. 总算 zǒngsuàn

表示经过相当长的时间或很大的努力才终于实现。例如:

It indicates that something eventually comes true after a rather long period of time or great effort. For example:

他们谈恋爱谈了5年,今年总算结婚了。

They have been in love for 5 years and they got married this year eventually.

我的汉语总算进步了。

My Chinese is improved eventually.

你总算来了!
You are here finally!

3. **于家中**　　yú jiā zhōng

"于"是介词,这里是"在"的意思,多用于书面语。例如:

"Yú" is a preposition, meaning "zài" here. It is mostly used in written Chinese. For example:

他出生于1956年,毕业于北京大学。

He was born in 1956 and graduated from Beijing University.

黄河发源于青海。

The Yellow River originates from Qinghai Province.

 **Exercises**

一　在括号中填上适当的补语　Fill in the blanks with proper complements.

1. 这张相片让我想(　　)了过去的事情。
2. 我已经爱(　　)了她,可是她不爱我。
3. 请关(　　)门。
4. 我要把握(　　)这次机会。
5. 我体会(　　)了爱情的甜蜜。

Lesson Ten A love letter

二 根据课文完成词语搭配 Complete the following word-collocations according to the text.

感到(　　　)　　(　　　)的感觉　　珍惜(　　　)
把握(　　　)　　体会到(　　　)　　充满(　　　)

三 选择填空 Choose the correct answers.

1. 我的汉语(　　)进步了,真不容易!
   A 一直　　B 还要　　C 总算　　D 没

2. 她(　　)地抚摸着他的脸。
   A 微笑　　B 思念　　C 爱　　D 温柔

3. 我(　　)地祝你幸福快乐!
   A 真诚　　B 痛苦　　C 微笑　　D 惊奇

四 选词填空 Fill in the following blanks with the proper words.

遥远　　眼前　　痛苦　　代替　　永远

1. 我不相信(　　　)的一切,这些都是真的吗?
2. 离婚以后他十分(　　　)。
3. 我们要(　　　)在一起!
4. 这个词可以(　　　)那个词吗?
5. 我的故乡在一个(　　　)的小山村。

相关阅读
Related Reading

（一）

Wéi:
维：

　　Ài de wéi, rúguǒ nǐ yě zhēn de zài ài wǒ, nǐ
　　爱 的 维，如 果 你 也 真 的 在 爱 我，你
yīnggāi huì gǎndào wǒ jīntiān yì tiān wèi nǐ fánnǎo de
应 该 会 感 到 我 今 天 一 天 为 你 烦 恼 的
xīn ba?
心 吧？

　　Zài ài de huǒ kāishǐ ránshāo de shíhou, jíshǐ
　　在 爱 的 火 开 始 燃 烧 的 时 候，即 使
zěnyàng kǔ, yě xiàng mì yíyàng de tián. Rú néng wèi nǐ fēng
怎 样 苦，也 像 蜜 一 样 的 甜。如 能 为 你 疯
chéng zhēn de kuángrén, wǒ shì zěnyàng de xìngfú; zhǐxiǎng wèi
成 真 的 狂 人，我 是 怎 样 的 幸 福；只 想 为
nǐ sǐqù hē!
你 死 去 呵！

　　Bù dài shuō wǒ zuìchū duì nǐ de ài jiù juéde yǒu-
　　不 待 说 我 最 初 对 你 的 爱 就 觉 得 有
diǎn qíguài, dàn nǐ bù yě shì tóngyàng ma? Wǒ qímiào de
点 奇 怪，但 你 不 也 是 同 样 吗？我 奇 妙 地
jiēshòule nǐ de jiēwěn. Dàn nà hé xiǎohái cóng cíài
接 受 了 你 的 接 吻。但 那 和 小 孩 从 慈 爱
de mǔqīn suǒ jiēshòu de yíyàng, bú shì nán nǚ liànqíng
的 母 亲 所 接 受 的 一 样，不 是 男 女 恋 情
de jiēwěn. Dàn wǒ de ài nǐ shì shēnshēn de, qiángliè de.
的 接 吻。但 我 的 爱 你 是 深 深 的，强 烈 的。

Lesson Ten A love letter

你好像从星的世界飞落来探寻我的心一样。

尝过种种痛苦的我,是不怕什么命运的,等,等,等几年几千万年的这种蠢念我不来。我生来是顽强,我要怎样就怎样,我还是任自己的心意行事吧。

维!愿你让我们的命运自然地转下去吧!

白薇

10.18

(节选自《昨夜》,上海南强书局,1933 年)

(二)

2003 年 5 月 23 日,我们结婚了!除了喜悦我只有喜悦。是你的爱让我走出

了对婚姻的恐惧,让我能开开心心地面对完全不同的生活。走进我们的房间,我就会感觉一股浓浓的爱的芳香扑面而来,像夏天清凉的海风,像冬天温暖的篝火!婚姻生活就是这样恬静而温馨,平淡而浪漫。总有说不完的话,总有诉不尽的情。随时随地都能感受到你的疼爱,随时随地都能品味爱情的甜蜜。我根本无法忍受和你的分离,即使只有17天,但对于我就有17个月那么长。我又一次体味到了相思的苦,又一次面对了牵挂的痛!两次分离,我一再地告诫自己要坚强,但我都失败了,因为我的生命中不能没有你,即使只是短暂的分离!

第11课 老太太唱情歌
Lesson Eleven The old ladies sing love songs

早晨，陪妈妈去公园做运动，才发现清晨的公园是如此热闹，有很多人在打拳、唱歌、跳舞，都是年纪大的老大爷和老太太。

妈妈感叹地说："这个世界倒过来了，老年人早早起来运动，小孩子

睡到太阳照屁股。"妈妈随即加入她的伙伴,在公园里舞动起来。我在园中散步,看到一些老先生老太太正动情地在唱卡拉OK,我就坐在旁边的石头上看着。

那些老先生、老太太唱歌的声音与神情深深地打动了我。他们的声音全都沙哑了,可他们的神情又是那样的专注与投入,夹带着非常深的感情。

有一位老太太唱到后来,泪流满面,使所有的人都因感动而沉默了。

是什么感情使老太太泪流满面呢?没有人问,也没有人知道。

Lesson Eleven　The old ladies sing love songs

　　Wǒ xiǎng, huódào mǒu ge niánjì de rén, yídìng
　　我 想，活 到 某 个 年 纪 的 人，一 定
dōu zài xīn zhōng yǐncángle xǔduō xǔduō zhēnqíng, zài
都 在 心 中 隐 藏 了 许 多 许 多 真 情，在
chànggē shí bèi chùdòng le.
唱 歌 时 被 触 动 了。

　　Wǒmen niánqīng de shíhou rúguǒ bù néng dòng-
　　我 们 年 轻 的 时 候 如 果 不 能 动
qíng de chàng yì shǒu qínggē, lǎo de shíhou yídìng yě bù
情 地 唱 一 首 情 歌，老 的 时 候 一 定 也 不
néng lèi liú mǎn miàn de chàng qínggē ba!
能 泪 流 满 面 地 唱 情 歌 吧!

　　　　　(xuǎn zì《Lín Qīngxuán Sǎnwén Jí》, yǒu shān gǎi)
　　　　　(选 自《林 清 玄 散 文 集》，有 删 改)

I accompanied my mother to a park on her exercises in the morning. I found that the park was so lively in the early morning. Many people were playing shadow boxing, singing, dancing, etc. All of them were old men and women.

My mother said with deep emotion, "The world is reversed. Old people do morning exercises in the early morning while children sleep late until the sun is shining on their asses." My mother joined her friends immediately and started dancing in the park. I took a walk in the park. I saw some old men and women were singing karaoke excitedly, and I sat on a nearby rock and watched them singing.

That singing and expressions on their faces touched me deeply. Their voices were husky, but they were so absorbed and devoted, to their singing.

One old lady shed floods of tears at the end of the singing. All the other people were moved by her and became quiet.

What kind of emotion moved her into tears? Nobody knew and no body asked.

I think people reaching a certain age must hide many true feelings in their hearts. They are touched when they sing songs.

If we can't sing love songs in our youth, we can't sing them with tears on our faces when we are old!

(Selected from the *Prose Collection of Lin Qingxuan*, adapted)

生 词 New Words

1. 老太太	lǎotàitai	(名)	old lady
2. 情歌	qínggē	(名)	love song
3. 陪	péi	(动)	accompany
4. 清晨	qīngchén	(名)	early morning
5. 如此	rúcǐ	(代)	so
6. 热闹	rènao	(形)	lively

Lesson Eleven　　The old ladies sing love songs

7. 跳舞	tiào//wǔ	（动）	dance
8. 年纪	niánjì	（名）	age
9. 老大爷	lǎodàye	（名）	(honorific) old man
10. 感叹	gǎntàn	（动）	sigh with feeling
11. 倒	dào	（动）	reverse
12. 太阳	tàiyáng	（名）	sun
13. 照	zhào	（动）	shine
14. 屁股	pìgu	（名）	ass
15. 随即	suíjí	（副）	immediately
16. 动情	dòng//qíng	（动）	become excited
17. 卡拉OK	kǎlā-OK		karaoke
18. 石头	shítou	（名）	stone
19. 神情	shénqíng	（名）	expression
20. 打动	dǎdòng	（动）	move
21. 沙哑	shāyǎ	（形）	husky
22. 专注	zhuānzhù	（形）	absorbed
23. 投入	tóurù	（动、形）	devote; devoted
24. 夹带	jiādài	（动）	carry with
25. 泪	lèi	（名）	tear
26. 沉默	chénmò	（形）	silent
27. 某	mǒu	（代）	some
28. 隐藏	yǐncáng	（动）	hide
29. 真情	zhēnqíng	（名）	true feeling
30. 触动	chùdòng	（动）	touch

 句 型 **Sentence Patterns**

1. 如此……

   清晨的公园是如此热闹。

   The park was so lively in the early morning.

   他对我如此热情,我都不好意思了。

   I felt embarrassed because he was so hospitable.

2. 随即……

   妈妈随即加入了她的伙伴,在公园里舞动起来。

   My mother joined her friends immediately and started dancing in the park.

   他走出大门,随即开车走了。

   He walked out of the gate and then drove away.

3. 满……

   他已经泪流满面了。

   His face was already full of tears.

满眼	eyeful	满屋子	houseful
满地	full of the field	满身	all over the body
满手	whole hand		

4. 因……而……

   她使所有的人都因感动而沉默了。

Lesson Eleven　The old ladies sing love songs

All the other people were moved by her and became quiet.

学校因放假而变得冷清了。

School became quiet because of holiday.

 注　释　Annotations

1. 活到某个年纪的人　*huódào mǒu ge niánjì de rén*

代词"某"表示不定指，用来指示不确定的人或物，有不愿意说或不需要说的含义。结构形式为：

The pronoun "mǒu" indicates a person or thing that is not known or not identified. It has the meaning of unwilling to say or needless to say. The basic patterns are:

1. 某 + 名词　　*mǒu* + noun

2. 某某 + 名词　　*mǒu mǒu* + noun

3. 某 + 量词 + 名词　　*mǒu* + measure word + noun

例如：某年某月的某一天　　某公司　　某男　　某地区

For example: on a certain date of a certain month of a certain year, a certain company, a certain man, a certain area

2. 带状语的句子　*dài zhuàngyǔ de jùzi*

老先生老太太正动情地在唱卡拉OK。

The old men and women were singing karaoke excitedly.

他们的神情深深地打动了我。

Chinese Crash Course

The expressions on the faces of old men and women touched me deeply.

我就坐在旁边的石头上看着。

I sat on a nearby rock and watched.

老的时候一定也不能泪流满面地唱情歌吧!

We can't sing love songs with tears on our faces when we are old!

 Exercises

一 根据课文，给下列句子加上适当的状语 Fill in the following blanks with proper adverbials according to the text.

1. 他们(　　)地唱着情歌。
2. 他(　　)地说:"真是太感谢你们了!"
3. 那些人(　　)地看老先生们唱京剧。

二 选择填空 Choose the correct answers.

1. 把这张图(　　)看一看,你会有新的发现。
   A 倒　　　B 倒起来　　　C 倒过来　　　D 倒下去
2. 她(　　)地唱着那首老歌。
   A 深深　　　B 感叹　　　C 触动　　　D 动情
3. 我(　　)这部电影感动得泪流满面。
   A 把　　　B 被　　　C 使　　　D 与

Lesson Eleven The old ladies sing love songs

三 选词填空 Fill in the following blanks with the proper words.

神情　投入　夹带　隐藏　触动

1. 这首歌曲（　　）了我的记忆。
2. 他的心里（　　）了很多秘密。
3. 他说汉语的时候还（　　）着很多英语。
4. 他表演的时候太（　　）了，到最后都忘了自己是在演戏。
5. 我喜欢看他沉默时的（　　）。

相关阅读
Related Reading

（一）

美丽的心

在一个演讲会上，一位听众问我："林先生，我发现来听你演讲的人，无论男女都长得很美丽。我想请问你，是美丽的人特别喜欢读你的书呢，还是读了你的书会变得美丽？"我说："你看到这些人这么美丽，那是因为你有美丽的心来看他们，就像现在我们看着你，

觉得你也十分美丽呀！"

演讲完后，我沿着公园走回家，发现在月色中的公园也非常的美丽。

是呀！这世界如此美丽，有的人特别容易看见，是缘于他们有美丽的心。

令人遗憾的是，通常我们只看见公园的美丽，花与树的美丽，月亮与星星的美丽，很少人去看别人的美丽，去看那在街头、在餐厅、在很多很多地方的许多美丽的心。

我的写作，不只是在告诉人关于这人间的美丽，而是在唤起一些沉睡着的美丽的心。

(选自《林清玄散文集》，有删改)

Lesson Eleven The old ladies sing love songs

(二)

李宇春登上最新一期《时代》亚洲版的封面,被杂志评为"勇敢、有胆量、执著及对当地其他人有勉励作用的亚洲英雄人物之一"。这一消息震动了整个华人娱乐圈,更令无数"超女粉丝"激动不已,认为这是给予李宇春及"超级女声"的至高荣誉。而近日在上海出席演唱会的李宇春却在排练间隙告诉记者,她曾拒绝接受《时代》的采访,也根本不知道自己竟会上封面。天娱公司也表示,他们没有接受过《时代》的采访,对这件事情感到非常"奇怪"。

《时代》在对李宇春的介绍中写道:"在中国,很少有电视明星能够像电影明星那样风光、受人瞩目。但是今年的八月却是一个例外。一个在湖南卫视播放的类似于"美国偶像"的节目在中国受到了热烈的欢迎,并成功地塑造出了一个受到万众瞩目的明星——21岁的四川学生李宇春。"《时代》认为,李宇春真正打动人的是她的态度,她的纯真,她对于中国传统的一种挑战,这些都是她的优势。

根据阅读内容判断正误:

1. 李宇春是通过一个电视节目而成为明星的。　　　(　)
2. 李宇春本人并不知道自己的照片被《时代》刊登出来。(　)
3. 李宇春是电影明星。　　　　　　　　　　　　　(　)

第 12 课 爸爸，您能听见吗
Lesson Twelve Dad, can you hear me

随着时间的流去，我记忆深处的父亲已经不再时常出现在我的梦中了，但是每次带着妻子女儿开车回故乡过春节，都要到爸爸的墓前去看一眼，跪在那里悄悄地说："爸爸，我回来了。"最近这几年，临走的时候也会去，说一声"爸爸，我走了"。这已成了我的习惯。

妈妈买了新房子，可是老房子总舍不得卖掉，我们都很怀念父亲，觉得我们一家人亲亲热热地在这里生活过，不能让别人来破坏。今年春节，

Chinese Crash Course

wǒ nále yàoshi, yí ge rén huídào bàba de shūfáng,
我拿了钥匙，一个人回到爸爸的书房，
kāishǐ fān yìxiē bàba de jiù shū xiǎng dàizǒu. Yǐqián
开始翻一些爸爸的旧书想带走。以前
shì bù gǎn de, pà zìjǐ jīnbuzhù liú lèi.
是不敢的，怕自己禁不住流泪。

　　Fāndào fùqin de yí ge xiǎo hézi, qīngqing de
　　翻到父亲的一个小盒子，轻轻地
dǎkāi, lǐmiàn shì hòuhòu de zhǐ, wǒ yóuyù le, rúguǒ
打开，里面是厚厚的纸，我犹豫了，如果
shì fùqin de xìnjiàn jiù bù hǎo le, dànshì hàoqíxīn
是父亲的信件就不好了，但是好奇心
shǐ wǒ háishi dǎkāi le.
使我还是打开了。

　　Nàxiē zhǐ quán shì wǒ de kǎoshì chéngjìdān hé
　　那些纸全是我的考试成绩单和
suǒyǒu de lùqǔ tōngzhīshū, cóng zhōngxué、dàxué dào
所有的录取通知书，从中学、大学到
yánjiūshēng, yì zhāng bù shǎo, yǒude bèimiàn hái yǒu bàba
研究生，一张不少，有的背面还有爸爸
de liúyán, wǒ rěnbuzhù kū le.
的留言，我忍不住哭了。

　　Bàba, měi cì wǒ shuō "wǒ huílai le" hé
　　爸爸，每次我说"我回来了"和
"wǒ zǒu le", gèng duō de shì xiǎng ràng nín bǎoyòu wǒ kāi
"我走了"，更多的是想让您保佑我开
chē píng'ān, dànshì zhè cì nín néng tīngjiàn ma?
车平安，但是这次您能听见吗？

Lesson Twelve Dad, can you hear me

With the passing of time, my father that lived in my memory does not appear in my dreams frequently any more. But each time when I drove my wife and daughter to my hometown and spend the Spring Festival, I wiuld go to visit my father's grave, kneeled down before it and said quietly, "Dad, I come back." In recent years, before my departure I also went there and said "Dad, I will leave." This has become my habit.

Mother bought a new house but she grudged selling the old house. We all miss our father. We don't want to let other people destroy it because we lived here happily for many years. In this Spring Festival I took the key, returned to my father's study and looked for some of my father's old books to take them away. I dared not to do this before because I was afraid that I found it difficult to hold back my tears.

I found a small box and opened it lightly. It was filled with papers. I hesitated a moment. If they were Father's private letters, it would be impolite. But my curiosity made me open it.

All of the papers were my school reports, admission notices to the middle school, college, and graduate school. They are all there with none missing. Some of the papers have my father's comments on it. I couldn't help crying.

Dad, each time I say "I come back" and "I am leaving", what I want more is to ask you to bless me to drive safely. But

Chinese Crash Course

this time, Dad, can you hear me?

1. 随着	suí zhe			with
随	suí	(动)		follow
2. 记忆	jìyì	(名)		memory
3. 时常	shícháng	(副)		frequently
4. 妻子	qīzi	(名)		wife
5. 墓	mù	(名)		tomb, grave
6. 跪	guì	(动)		kneel down
7. 悄悄	qiāoqiāo	(副)		quietly
8. 临	lín	(介)		about to
9. 总	zǒng	(副)		always
10. 舍不得	shěbude	(动)		hate to part with
11. 怀念	huáiniàn	(动)		miss
12. 亲热	qīnrè	(形)		intimate
13. 破坏	pòhuài	(动)		destroy
14. 钥匙	yàoshi	(名)		key
15. 书房	shūfáng	(名)		study
16. 翻	fān	(动)		look for
17. 旧	jiù	(形)		old

Lesson Twelve Dad, can you hear me

18. 敢	gǎn	(助动)	dare	
19. 禁不住	jīnbuzhù	(动)	cannot help	
20. 盒子	hézi	(名)	box	
21. 厚	hòu	(形)	thick	
22. 纸	zhǐ	(名)	paper	
23. 犹豫	yóuyù	(动)	hesitate	
24. 好奇心	hàoqíxīn	(名)	curiosity	
好奇	hàoqí	(形)	curious	
25. 录取	lùqǔ	(动)	enroll	
26. 研究生	yánjiūshēng	(名)	graduate student	
27. 背面	bèimiàn	(名)	back	
28. 留言	liúyán	(名)	message	
29. 忍	rěn	(动)	endure	
30. 保佑	bǎoyòu	(动)	bless	
31. 平安	píng'ān	(形)	safe	

 **Sentence Patterns**

1. 随着……

随着时间的流去,我记忆深处的父亲已经不再时常出现在我的梦中了。

With the passing of time, my father that lived in my memory does not appear in my dreams frequently any more.

随着经济的发展,人们的文化生活也不断丰富起来。

With the development of economy, people's cultural life has also become rich and colorful.

2. 临……

临走的时候也会去父亲的墓上看一眼。

When I left, I also went to visit my father's grave.

临上飞机前,我才想起忘记了一样东西。

I remember something was left out just before boarding the airplane.

3. 总……

妈妈总舍不得卖掉老房子。

Mother grudged selling the old house.

你怎么总迟到?

Why are you late so often?

4. 禁不住……

我怕自己禁不住流下眼泪。

I was afraid that I found it difficult to hold back my tears.

他禁不住哈哈大笑起来。

He couldn't help laughing loudly.

Lesson Twelve Dad, can you hear me

注 释 Annotations

1. 随着   suí zhe

"随"是动词,表示伴随,常带"着",后接名词做句子的状语。例如:

"Suí" is a verb, indicating concomitance and is always followed by "zhe". It is followed by a noun acting as the adverbial of a sentence. For example:

随着市场需求的变化,汽车保险业也应该改革。

With the changing need of market, auto insurance also should reform.

让我们随着音乐跳舞吧!

Let's dance to the music.

心中的痛苦会随着时间慢慢减弱的。

The pain in mind may weaken slowly as time flows away.

2. 总舍不得   zǒng shěbude

"总"也可以说成"总是",后接动词时表示行为一直不变。例如:

"Zǒng" or "zǒngshì", when followed by a verb, indicates the action remains unchanged. For example:

每天下午他们总是来这个公园唱京剧。

They always come to this park to sing Beijing opera every afternoon.

他总是不听我的。

He doesn't listen to me all the time.

这个城市总是下雨。

It rains in this city.

Chinese Crash Course

练习 Exercises

一　根据课文完成词语搭配 Complete the following word-collocations according to the text.

记忆(　　　)　　　怀念(　　　　)　　　禁不住(　　　　)
(　　)通知书　　　轻轻地(　　　　)　　　保佑(　　　　)

二　选择填空 Choose the correct answers.

1. (　　)走的时候,他送了我一件礼物。
   A 随着　　　B 临　　　C 总算　　　D 终于
2. 我不想告诉她这件事,可是又(　　)给她打了电话。
   A 忍住　　　B 忍不起　　　C 忍不住　　　D 忍下去
3. 孩子都有很强的(　　)。
   A 好奇　　　B 奇怪　　　C 奇怪心　　　D 好奇心
4. 这些孩子都找到了,(　　)个不少。
   A 所有　　　B 都　　　C 某　　　D 一

三　选词填空 Fill in the following blanks with the proper words.

悄悄　　亲热　　禁不住　　犹豫　　平安

1. 选择哪个计划,我(　　)了很长时间。
2. 祝你旅途(　　)!
3. 他(　　)地对我说:"你千万不要告诉别人!"
4. 一家人能(　　)地坐在一起吃晚饭,这就是幸福!
5. 人们(　　)要问:"这场比赛我们为什么没有准备好?"

Lesson Twelve　Dad, can you hear me

相关阅读
Related Reading

（一）

Fùqin qùshì èrshí nián le, mǔqin bǎ wǒmen
父亲去世20年了，母亲把我们
yǎngyù chéngrén, kě xiànzài wǒmen dōu jié le hūn, líkāile
养育成人，可现在我们都结了婚，离开了
tā. Měi cì huíqu tā zǒng shì gěi wǒmen zuò chīde,
她。每次回去她总是给我们做吃的，
suīrán hěn máng, dàn tèbié gāoxìng.
虽然很忙，但特别高兴。

　　Qùnián Chūn Jié, wǒ hé zhàngfu dàizhe háizi huí
　　去年春节，我和丈夫带着孩子回
lǎojiā hé mǔqin yìqǐ guònián. Gāng yí xià qìchē, yuǎn-
老家和母亲一起过年。刚一下汽车，远
yuǎn de jiù kànjiàn mǔqin zhànzài jiā ménqián wàngzhe wǒmen
远地就看见母亲站在家门前望着我们
lái de fāngxiàng, huābái de tóufa zài fēngxuě zhōng piāodòng.
来的方向，花白的头发在风雪中飘动。
Wǒ bízi yì suān, yǎnlèi jīnbuzhù liúle chulai. Xiǎng-
我鼻子一酸，眼泪禁不住流了出来。想
dào mǔqin yì rén shēnghuó, yídìng hěn jìmò, wǒ jiù gǎn-
到母亲一人生活，一定很寂寞，我就感
dào duìbuqǐ mǔqin, gǎndào zìjǐ méiyou jìndào nǚ'ér de
到对不起母亲，感到自己没有尽到女儿的
zérèn. Yào huí Běijīng le, wǒ qǐng mǔqin gēn wǒ yìqǐ
责任。要回北京了，我请母亲跟我一起
huíqu, tā bú yuànyì, shuō: "Bié dānxīn, yǒu shíjiān duō
回去，她不愿意，说："别担心，有时间多

Chinese Crash Course

xiě wénzhāng jì huilai."
写 文 章 寄 回 来。"

　　Mǔqin bǎ wǒ jìhuí de wénzhāng dōu fàngzàile yí ge
　　母 亲 把 我 寄 回 的 文 章 都 放 在 了 一 个
hézi li, zhè hézi zhuāngmǎnle mǔqin duì wǒ de ài,
盒 子 里，这 盒 子 装 满 了 母 亲 对 我 的 爱，
yě yǒu wǒ duì tā de ài.
也 有 我 对 她 的 爱。

　　根据阅读内容判断正误：

　　1. 母亲住在北京，我住在外地。　　　　　　　　（　　）
　　2. 母亲只想看我的文章，不愿意跟我们住在一起。（　　）
　　3. 我们春节看母亲，母亲很高兴。　　　　　　　（　　）

　　　　　　　　　　（二）

　　Yǒuguān rénshì yánjiū biǎomíng, Zhōngguó de jiātíng
　　有 关 人 士 研 究 表 明，中 国 的 家 庭
jiàoyù zhèngzài chūxiàn "yán mǔ cí fù" de zhuàngkuàng. Sūn Yún-
教 育 正 在 出 现 "严 母 慈 父" 的 状 况。孙 云
xiǎo jièshào, háizi duì fùmǔ de qínggǎn yào jīnglì wǔ
晓 介 绍，孩 子 对 父 母 的 情 感 要 经 历 五
ge zhǔyào jiēduàn: shí suì yǐqián yǐ chóngbài wéi zhǔ;
个 主 要 阶 段：10 岁 以 前 以 崇 拜 为 主；
shí suì dào èrshí suì shí, zhè zhǒng gǎnqíng zhuǎnwéi qīngshì;
10 岁 到 20 岁 时，这 种 感 情 转 为 轻 视；
èrshí suì dào sānshí suì, háizi duì fùmǔ yǒule yìxiē
20 岁 到 30 岁，孩 子 对 父 母 有 了 一 些
lǐjiě; sānshí suì dào sìshí suì shí háizi duì fùmǔ duōle
理 解；30 岁 到 40 岁 时 孩 子 对 父 母 多 了

Lesson Twelve Dad, can you hear me

一些爱；40岁以后孩子才能真正深刻地理解父母。而很多母亲的焦虑期正好碰上了孩子的轻视期。

"我们也很委屈，为孩子做了这么多，在孩子眼里却成了'坏人'，平时对孩子不管不问的孩子的爸爸却成了'好人'。"周女士说。"母亲已经成了现在这个社会中最为焦虑的群体。"孙云晓认为。女性除了在家庭中承担着更多的持家和教养孩子的压力外，随着整个社会生存压力的增大，她们还要与男性一样承担着职业的压力，因此，她们的焦虑程度也在明显地增大。

根据阅读内容判断正误：

1. 很多母亲对孩子不好，而父亲却对孩子好。   (　)
2. 母亲的焦虑有很多复杂的社会原因。   (　)
3. 10岁以前的孩子一般很难理解母亲的管教。   (　)

第13课 中国的流动人口与人口流动

Lesson Thirteen Chinese floating population and population flow

根据中国的户口制度,没有本地户口的外来人员就是外来人口,城市中的外来人口大多是农民,我们也叫流动人口。

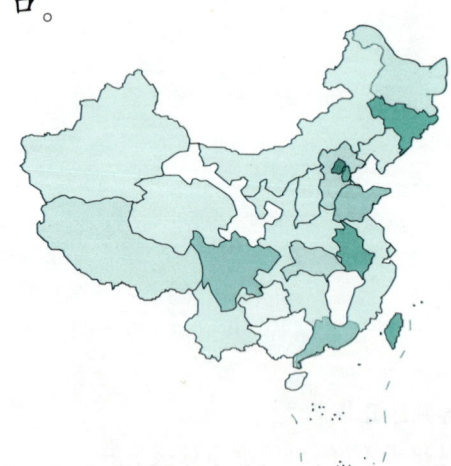

Lesson Thirteen Chinese floating population and population flow

中国改革开放以后，粮食问题已经解决，这对一个发展中的人口大国来说，是一个惊人的成绩。农民希望缩小城乡差别，便进入城市来打工。他们中有些长期居住者就变成了外来人口，中国因此就有了流动人口问题。在北京、上海和广州这样的大城市里，外来人口占20%，这么多的外来人口给大城市带来了负担，但是流动人口的积极作用是巨大的。首先人口流动活跃了经济，外来人口为城市提供了大量的劳动力；其次，人口流动使人们在观念上互相交流、补充。因为中国地区差异很明显，各地都有

Chinese Crash Course

yōudiǎn érqiě fāzhǎn hěn bu pínghéng. Yǐqián rénmen
优点而且发展很不平衡。以前人们
cháng shuō běifāngrén ài miànzi ér nánfāngrén shànyú
常说北方人爱面子而南方人善于
jīngshāng, jìnrù shìchǎng jīngjì yǐhòu, zhèyàng shuō jiù bú
经商，进入市场经济以后，这样说就不
zhèngquè le.
正确了。

　　Rénkǒu de liúdòng dàilái jīngjì fāzhǎn de
　　人口的流动带来经济发展的
huólì, wǒmen xīwàng rénkǒu bùjǐn shì nóngcūn xiàng
活力，我们希望人口不仅是农村向
chéngshì liúdòng, yě xīwàng shì chéngshì xiàng chéngshì、chéngshì
城市流动，也希望是城市向城市、城市
xiàng nóngcūn liúdòng, dào nàshí wǒmen kàndào de jiù bú
向农村流动，到那时我们看到的就不
shì zāng、luàn、chà de shèhuì wèntí le, érshì réncái de
是脏、乱、差的社会问题了，而是人才的
zìyóu liúdòng hé rénmen duì shēnghuó de zìyóu xuǎnzé.
自由流动和人们对生活的自由选择。

　　According to Chinese system of registered permanent residence, the ones who don't have local registered permanent residence are non-native. Most non-natives in the cities are farmers; we also call them floating population.

　　After China's reform and opening up, the problem of grain has been solved. It is a surprising achievement for a developing country with a large population. The farmers hope to narrow the

Lesson Thirteen Chinese floating population and population flow

gap between city and country, and then they come into the cities to do manual work. Some who reside in the cities for a long period of time become non-natives. Thus China has the problem of a floating population. The non-native account for 20% of the population in total in big cities such as Beijing, Shanghai and Guangzhou. Though such a large floating population brings heavy burden to these cities, the positive role of the floating population cannot be overlooked. Firstly, population flow activates the economy and the non-native provide a large amount of labor force for the cities. Secondly, population flow makes people communicate and complement each other in concept. Because the regional disparity is very obvious in China, each place has its own advantage and the development is not balanced. People used to say that northerners are sensitive about their reputation while southerners are good at doing business. This conclusion is not correct after we enter the market economy.

Population flow brings vitality to the economic development. We hope that population does not only flow from country to city but also among cities and from city to country. At that time, we will not see the social problems of dirtiness, disorder and poverty, but the free flow of talented people and the free choice that people have for their life.

Chinese Crash Course

生　词　New Words

1. 流动	liúdòng	（动）	flow
2. 人口	rénkǒu	（名）	population
3. 户口	hùkǒu	（名）	registered permanent residence
4. 制度	zhìdù	（名）	system
5. 农民	nóngmín	（名）	farmer
6. 粮食	liángshi	（名）	food, grain
7. 惊人	jīngrén	（形）	suprising
8. 缩小	suōxiǎo	（动）	reduce
9. 便	biàn	（副）	so
10. 进入	jìnrù	（动）	enter
11. 打工	dǎ//gōng	（动）	do a temporary job
12. 长期	chángqī	（名）	long term
13. 负担	fùdān	（动、名）	shoulder; burden
14. 作用	zuòyòng	（名）	effect
15. 首先	shǒuxiān	（副、连）	first; first of all
16. 活跃	huóyuè	（动、形）	activate; brisk
17. 提供	tígōng	（动）	provide
18. 大量	dàliàng	（形）	abundant

Lesson Thirteen Chinese floating population and population flow

19.	其次	qícì	（代）	secondly
20.	交流	jiāoliú	（动）	communicate
21.	补充	bǔchōng	（动）	complement
22.	差异	chāyì	（名）	difference, disparity
23.	明显	míngxiǎn	（形）	distinct
24.	优点	yōudiǎn	（名）	advantage
25.	平衡	pínghéng	（形）	balanced
26.	北方人	běifāngrén	（名）	northerner
27.	面子	miànzi	（名）	reputation
28.	南方人	nánfāngrén	（名）	southerner
29.	善于	shànyú	（动）	be good at
30.	市场经济	shìchǎng jīngjì		market economy
31.	活力	huólì	（名）	energy
32.	脏	zāng	（形）	dirty
33.	乱	luàn	（形）	disorderly
34.	人才	réncái	（名）	talented people

 句　型 Sentence Patterns

1. 大多是……

城市中的外来人口大多是农民。

Most of the non-natives in the cities are farmers.

目前在北京的留学生大多是韩国人。

At present most of the foreign students in Beijing are from South Korea.

2. 缩小……差别

农民希望缩小城乡差别。

The farmers hope to narrow the gap between city and country.

我们要大力发展科技,以缩小和发达国家的差别。

We need to devote our great efforts to develop science and technology so as to narrow the gap with developed countries.

3. 便……

农民希望缩小城乡差别,便进入城市来打工。

The farmers hope to narrow the gap between city and country, and then they come into the cities to do manual work.

他想查点儿资料,便去了图书馆。

He wanted to check some information, so he went to the library.

4. 首先,……;其次,……

首先,人口流动活跃了经济;其次,人口流动使人们在观念上互相交流、补充。

Firstly, population flow activates the economy; secondly, it makes people communicate and complement each other in concept.

这个国家的改革,首先是改变人们的观念,其次是改变制度。

The reform of this country is first to change people's concept, and

Lesson Thirteen　Chinese floating population and population flow

then to change the system.

5. 善于……

南方人善于经商。

Southerners are good at doing business.

他很善于跟别人交流。

He is very good at communicating with other people.

 注　释　**Annotation**

便进入城市来打工　　*biàn jìnrù chéngshì lái dǎgōng*

"便"是副词,相当于"就",这里表示行为的顺接关系。例如:

"Biàn" is an adverb which is equivalent to "jiù". It indicates consecutive relationship of actions. For example:

我很想跟她谈谈,便给她打了电话约她吃饭。

I would like very much to talk to her, so I called her and invited her to dinner.

周末休息,他便带着孩子去了公园。

He took his kid to the park because he rests at the weekend.

看到情况发生了变化,他便改变了原来的计划。

He changed his original plan when he saw the changes of conditions.

一 根据课文完成词语搭配 Complete the following word-collocations according to the text.

( )制度　　　　人口( )　　　　惊人的( )

缩小( )　　　　( )作用　　　　活跃( )

提供( )　　　　差异( )　　　　善于( )

二 选择填空 Choose the correct answers.

1. 解决粮食问题( )发展中国家很重要。

　A 和　　　　B 跟　　　　C 与　　　　D 对

2. 农民为了缩小城乡差别,( )进入城市打工。

　A 还　　　　B 便　　　　C 和　　　　D 还有

3. 他很( )做生意,我们应该多跟他合作。

　A 善于　　　B 强　　　　C 要　　　　D 优点

三 注意下列词的词性,并用它们不同的词性分别造句 Pay attention to the parts of speech of the following words and make sentences with them respectively.

例如:规定:我们规定早八点上课。　　(动词)

　　　　我们应该遵守规定。　　　　(名词)

Lesson Thirteen Chinese floating population and population flow

活跃 （   ）（动词）
     （   ）（形容词）

首先 （   ）（副词）
     （   ）（连词）

计划 （   ）（名词）
     （   ）（动词）

投入 （   ）（形容词）
     （   ）（动词）

相关阅读
Related Reading

（一）

Shìchǎng jīngjì gǎibiànle wǒmen de shēnghuó guānniàn,
市 场 经 济 改 变 了 我 们 的 生 活 观 念，
nóngmín yě kěyǐ zài chéngshì lìyè, zhèxiē wàilái rénkǒu
农 民 也 可 以 在 城 市 立 业，这 些 外 来 人 口
cóng shúxi chéngshì dào jiēshòu xīn guānniàn huò dào zài huí
从 熟 悉 城 市 到 接 受 新 观 念 或 到 再 回
nóngcūn gàn zìjǐ de chǎnyè, tāmen yǒude chéngwéi dà
农 村 干 自 己 的 产 业，他 们 有 的 成 为 大
lǎobǎn, yǒude chéngwéi chǎo gǔ zhuānjiā, hái yǒude chéngwéi-
老 板，有 的 成 为 炒 股 专 家，还 有 的 成 为
le qǐyèjiā.
了 企 业 家。

Chinese Crash Course

以北京为例，一般的日常服务行业如餐饮、服装加工、贩卖、各类小商品市场，80%是外来人口经营的，没有人口流动是不可能实现经济多样化的。

现在，政府每年设立"优秀外来人员奖"，鼓励他们的创业精神；解决他们的实际问题——如政府帮助外来人口就业，免费进行职业培训；管理上办理外来人口暂住证……这些措施都是为了促进农村和城市经济的共同繁荣。

根据阅读内容判断正误：

1. 北京人喜欢做普通的服务行业。　　　　　　（　　）
2. 政府鼓励外来人员在大城市就业。　　　　　（　　）
3. 人口流动对城市和农村的经济发展都有好处。（　　）

Lesson Thirteen Chinese floating population and population flow

(二)

据辽宁省农委调查,目前全省有农村劳动力1016万人,外出务工的农村劳动力达286万人,其中常年在外务工人员140万人,尚有730万人驻留农村从事第一产业。按照一般经营规模,还有近200万农村劳动力需要转移培训。为此,辽宁加大了农村劳动力转移培训的力度,2005年全省农村劳动力转移职业技能培训补贴标准为平均每人260元,比上年增加30%。

当前辽宁正处在老工业基地振兴的快速发展时期,工业化、城镇化和农业现代化的发展为转移农村富余

劳动力、发展劳务经济提供了广阔空间。辽宁省农业部门正加强对农村劳动力转移培训的管理,确保"输出一人,致富一家,带动一方"。

根据阅读内容判断正误:

1. 辽宁省只有10%的农村劳动力外出打工。　　　　(　)
2. 辽宁省政府帮助农民学习技能,使他们出去后有更好的工作能力。　　　　(　)
3. 政府在培训农民技能方面花费了很多钱。　　　　(　)

第 14 课 新闻
Lesson Fourteen News

记者今日从公安部出入境管理局了解到,简化台湾居民来往大陆入出境和在大陆居留手续的措施于7月25日正式实施。这个措施放宽了台湾居民来往大陆的有效期限,也放宽了次数的限制,在大陆的台湾居民可以申请1年内一次或多次来往大陆。据记者了解,从1987年11月开始,公安机关出入境管理部门不断简化台湾居民来往大陆的手续,促进了两岸人员往来和经济、文化等领域的交流。台湾居民

Chinese Crash Course

来大陆由最早的探亲、旅游逐渐扩大到投资、经商以及教育、科学、文化、医疗、体育等交流活动。据统计,自1987年至2004年,台湾居民来大陆超过3388万人次。2005年上半年,台湾居民来大陆超过200万人次,创造了历史最高纪录。

(本文发表时间:2005/7/25)

    Today, reporters got news from the Entry and Exit Administration Bureau of the Ministry of Public Security that the measure of simplifying the procedures of Taiwan compatriots entering or leaving the mainland of China and residing in it will be put into effect formally on 25, July.

    This measure relaxes the restriction of valid time limit for Taiwan compatriots to come and leave the mainland of China. It also relaxes the restriction of times. A Taiwan resident living in the mainland of China can apply for one time or several times to come or leave in one year. As far as the reporter knows, from November, 1987 to the present, that the Entry and Exit Admin-

Lesson Fourteen News

istration Bureau of the Ministry of Public Security has kept on simplifiying the procedures for Taiwan compatriots to come and leave the mainland of China. It facilitates the communica-

tion between Chinese people and promotes economic and cultural exchanges across the Taiwan Straits. Taiwan compatriots came to China's mainland from visiting their relatives or sightseeing in the very beginning, gradually to making investment, doing business, and promoting educational, scientific, cultural, medical and sporting exchanges. According to the statistics from 1987 to 2004, the number of Taiwan compatriots coming to the mainland of China exceeded 33.88 million. In the first half of 2005, the number of Taiwan compatriots coming into China's mainland has exceeded 2 million people, which has created a historical record.

(This article is published at July 25th, 2005)

Chinese Crash Course

生　词　New Words

1. 新闻	xīnwén	（名）	news
2. 记者	jìzhě	（名）	reporter
3. 出入境	chū-rùjìng		entry and exit
4. 简化	jiǎnhuà	（动）	simplify
5. 来往	láiwǎng	（动）	come and leave
6. 大陆	dàlù	（名）	mainland of China
7. 入出境	rù-chūjìng		exit and entry
8. 手续	shǒuxù	（名）	procedure
9. 措施	cuòshī	（名）	measure
10. 正式	zhèngshì	（形）	formal
11. 实施	shíshī	（动）	put into effect
12. 放宽	fàngkuān	（动）	relax
13. 有效	yǒuxiào	（形）	valid
14. 期限	qīxiàn	（名）	time limit
15. 申请	shēnqǐng	（动）	apply
16. 不断	búduàn	（副）	constantly
17. 促进	cùjìn	（动）	facilitate
18. 两岸	liǎng'àn	（名）	both sides across the Taiwan Straits

Lesson Fourteen News

19. 领域	lǐngyù	(名)	field	
20. 由	yóu	(介)	from	
21. 探亲	tàn//qīn	(动)	go home and visit one's family	
22. 逐渐	zhújiàn	(副)	gradually	
23. 扩大	kuòdà	(动)	expand	
24. 以及	yǐjí	(连)	as well as	
25. 教育	jiàoyù	(名)	education	
26. 科学	kēxué	(名)	science	
27. 医疗	yīliáo	(名)	medical treatment	
28. 体育	tǐyù	(名)	sports	
29. 人次	réncì	(量)	(*measure word*) person-time	
30. 创造	chuàngzào	(动)	create	
31. 纪录	jìlù	(名)	record	
32. 发表	fābiǎo	(动)	publish	

专有名词 **Proper Nouns**

1. 公安部   Gōng'ān Bù   Ministry of Public Security
2. 出入境管理局   Chū-rùjìng Guǎnlǐ Jú   Entry and Exit Administration Bureau

3. 台湾　　　　　Táiwān　　　　　Taiwan (Province)

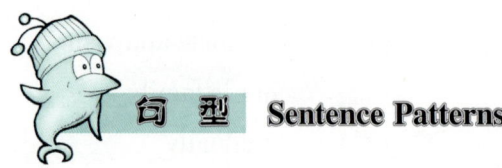 **Sentence Patterns**

1. 于……实施

简化台湾居民来往大陆入出境手续的措施于 7 月 25 日正式实施。

The measure of simplifying the procedures of Taiwan compatriots entering or leaving the mainland of China and residing in it will be put into effect formally on 25, July.

政府制定的交通法令于今日 5 点起开始实施。

The traffic law formulated by the government comes into force from 5 o'clock today.

2. 促进……

简化台湾居民来大陆的手续促进了两岸的经济和文化交流。

Simplifying the procedures of Taiwan compatriots coming to the mainland of China facilitates economic and cultural exchanges across the Taiwan Straits.

文化交流也可以促进经济交流。

Cultural exchange can also facilitate economic cooperation.

3. 由……

台湾居民来大陆由最早的探亲扩大到投资、经商等活动。

Lesson Fourteen　News

Taiwan compatriots coming to the mainland of China have expanded their activities from visiting their relatives or sightseeing in the very beginning to making investment and doing business.

他们公司已经由一个15人的小公司发展成了一个500多人的大公司。

Their company has developed from a small company with 15 people into a big company with more than 500 people.

4. 以及……

来大陆的目的由探亲扩大到投资、经商以及教育、科学、文化等交流活动。

Their purposes of coming to the mainland of China expand from visiting their relatives, or sightseeing to making investment, doing business and promoting educational, scientific and cultural exchanges.

他们的产品卖到了中国香港、新加坡以及欧美等地。

Their products is sold to China's Hong Kong, Singapore, Europe and America, etc.

 **注　释　Annotation**

由　　*yóu*

介词"由"有"从"的意思，可以表示时间的起点，跟时间词语结合。例如：

The preposition "*yóu*" has the meaning of "*cóng*". It can indicate the starting point of time and is used together with time words and expressions. For example:

我们的工作由早九点开始,到晚八点结束。

Our work begins from 9 o'clock in the morning and ends at 8 o'clock in the evening.

将由明年开始实施这个制度。

This system will be carried out next year.

在课文里"由"表示发展、变化或范围的起点。例如:

"Yóu" in the text indicates the starting point of development, change or range. For example:

他由一个小男孩长成大小伙子了。

He grows up to be a young man from a little boy.

杯子里的水由无色变成了红色,又由红色变成了绿色。

The water in the glass turned from colorless into red and then from red into green.

中国已经由计划经济时期发展到了市场经济时期。

China has developed from the period of planned economy into the one of market economy.

练习 Exercises

一 根据课文完成词语搭配 Complete the following word-collocations according to the text.

从( )了解到　　简化( )　　正式( )

Lesson Fourteen News

实施(　　)　　　　放宽(　　)　　　　促进(　　)

(　　)领域　　　　超过(　　)　　　　创造(　　)

二　选择填空　Choose the correct answers.

1. 我们现在使用的汉字是简体字,就是经过(　　)的汉字。
   A 简单　　　B 实施　　　C 简化　　　D 措施

2. 政府的措施(　　)了对外的贸易交流。
   A 放宽　　　B 简化　　　C 解决　　　D 促进

3. 我们(　　)收到各地关心我们节目的观众的邮件。
   A 正在　　　B 逐渐　　　C 不断　　　D 很多

4. 完成这个工作的最后(　　)是什么时候?
   A 期限　　　B 限制　　　C 时期　　　D 时间

5. 我们的合作领域扩大(　　)科学技术方面。
   A 到　　　　B 上　　　　C 了　　　　D 着

三　把下列词语组合成句子　Rearrange the following words and phrases into sentences.

1. 实施了　措施　公安部　新的

2. 我们双方　这个措施　交流　经济和科学文化的　促进了

3. 文化领域　由　扩大到　经济领域　我们的合作

相关阅读
Related Reading

（一）

据新华社专电，美国《福布斯》杂志2005年7月28日公布了第二届年度"世界百强女性风云榜"。美国国务卿康多莉扎·赖斯再度名列榜首，当选为全球最具影响力女性。中国副总理吴仪位列第二。

菲律宾总统阿罗约由去年的第九名跃升五位，排名第四。风云榜上，商海女杰中排位最靠前的，是玛格丽特·惠特曼，E-bay（电子港湾）首席执行官，位列第五。紧随其后的是施乐公司首席执行官安妮·马尔卡希。美国"脱口秀"女王进入前十名，位列第九。

Lesson Fourteen News

畅销书《哈里·波特》的作者J·K·罗琳，排名第四十位。《福布斯》称，排行榜是候选者在全球媒体被提及的次数、在经济领域的影响力两项相加的结果。

根据阅读内容判断正误：

1. 《福布斯》的排名标准是根据女性的外貌。　　（　）
2. 这次排名里面没有女性作家。　　　　　　　（　）
3. 菲律宾女总统的影响力在上升。　　　　　　（　）

（二）

2005年10月，神舟六号载人飞船升空，东方时空和新浪网联合推出调查：您向往太空旅行吗？以下为部分调查内容。

1. 神舟六号飞船发射前，您最关心什么？
   ○ 飞船发射的确切时间
   ○ 航天员是谁

- 飞船携带什么特殊物品
- 航天员的太空生活
- 航天员在太空进行何种试验
- 运载火箭技术

2. 您认为这次宇航员在太空中最困难的是什么？
- 解决吃喝拉撒睡
- 做科学试验
- 两个人配合工作
- 克服寂寞、孤独等心理不适
- 其他

3. 您渴望到太空旅行吗？
- 很渴望
- 不想去
- 说不好，没想过

第 15 课 普通话与方言
Dì Shíwǔ Kè Pǔtōnghuà yǔ Fāngyán

Lesson Fifteen *Putonghua* and dialects

Xuéxí Hànyǔ de pǔtōnghuà, bù kě bìmiǎn de yào jiēchù dào gè dì fāngyán. Hànyǔ zìgǔ jiù yǒu fāngyán de fēnqí, érqiě Hàn mínzú lìshǐ yōujiǔ, rénkǒu zhòngduō, fēnbù guǎngfàn, fāngyán de xiànxiàng jiù biàn de hěn fùzá.

学习汉语的普通话，不可避免地要接触到各地方言。汉语自古就有方言的分歧，而且汉民族历史悠久，人口众多，分布广泛，方言的现象就变得很复杂。

Xiàndài Hànyǔ kěyǐ fēn wéi qī dà fāngyánqū: Běifāng fāngyán、Wú fāngyán、Xiāng fāngyán、Gàn fāngyán、Kèjiā fāngyán、Mǐn fāngyán hé Yuè fāngyán. Qízhōng Běifāng fāngyán yǐ Běijīnghuà wéi dàibiǎo, nèibù bǐjiào yízhì, shǐyòng rénkǒu zhàn Hànzú zǒng rénkǒu de bǎi fēn zhī qīshísān.

现代汉语可以分为七大方言区：北方方言、吴方言、湘方言、赣方言、客家方言、闽方言和粤方言。其中北方方言以北京话为代表，内部比较一致，使用人口占汉族总人口的73%。

Hàn mínzú de gòngtóngyǔ —— pǔtōnghuà yǐ Běifāng fāngyán wéi jīchǔ, yǐ Běijīng yǔyīn wéi biāozhǔnyīn.

汉民族的共同语——普通话以北方方言为基础，以北京语音为标准音。

Chinese Crash Course

从语音、词汇、语法系统与普通话的差别来看，闽、粤方言与普通话距离最大。客家、闽、粤方言是华侨中使用最多的方言。

世界上一般国家、民族都不同程度地重视、推广共同语和标准语，以使社会交际变得方便。新中国成立后，几十年来国家一直致力于推广

Lesson Fifteen Putonghua and dialects

pǔtōnghuà, zhè shì guójiā tǒngyī、 mínzú tuánjié、
普 通 话，这 是 国 家 统 一、民 族 团 结、
shèhuì jìnbù de xūyào, shì jiāojì de xūyào.
社 会 进 步 的 需 要，是 交 际 的 需 要。
Zhèngzhì shēnghuó、 jīngjì shēnghuó、 wénhuà shēnghuó hé
政 治 生 活、经 济 生 活、文 化 生 活 和
shèhuì shēnghuó dōu bù néng méiyǒu pǔtōnghuà, guójiā
社 会 生 活 都 不 能 没 有 普 通 话，国 家
dāngrán yīngdāng zhòngshì bìng jiāqiáng tuīguǎng pǔtōnghuà,
当 然 应 当 重 视 并 加 强 推 广 普 通 话，
shǐ pǔtōnghuà zài shèhuì yǔyán shēnghuó zhōng fāhuī
使 普 通 话 在 社 会 语 言 生 活 中 发 挥
zhòngyào zuòyòng.
重 要 作 用。

It is inevitable to bring you into contact with many dialects when you learn *Putonghua* (standard Chinese). The Chinese language has had different dialects since ancient times. And also the Han nationality language has a long history, with a large and widely-distributed population. Thus the phenomena of dialects are very complicated.

The modern Chinese can be divided into seven dialect districts: North, Wu, Xiang, Gan, Hakka, Min and Yue. Among them Beijing accent is the representative of the North dialects. They are consistent with themselves. The number of the people who speak north dialects accounts for 73% of the Han nationality's population. The common language of the Han nationality — *Putonghua* is based on the North dialects and takes the Beijing accent as the standard pronunciation.

To see from the differences in pronunciation, vocabulary and grammar system, Min and Yue dialects have the greatest difference from *Putonghua*. Hakka, Min and Yue dialects are the ones that are mostly used among overseas Chinese.

Most countries and nationalities in the world all pay attention to popular common language and standard pronunciation at various degrees to make social communication more convenient. Since the People's Republic of China was founded, the government has been dedicated to popularize *Putonghua* for dozens of years. It is the needs of the country's unification, ethnic solidarity and social progress. It is also the demand for communication. Political, economic, cultural and social lives cannot be carried out without *Putonghua*. The government should attach importance and promote the popularition of *Putonghua*, and make it play an important role in social language life.

Lesson Fifteen   Putonghua and dialects

生 词   New Words

1. 普通话	pǔtōnghuà	（名）	*Putonghua* (standard Chinese)
2. 方言	fāngyán	（名）	dialect
3. 避免	bìmiǎn	（动）	avoid
4. 分歧	fēnqí	（名）	difference
5. 众多	zhòngduō	（形）	numerous
6. 分布	fēnbù	（动）	distribute
7. 广泛	guǎngfàn	（形）	wide
8. 内部	nèibù	（名）	interior
9. 一致	yízhì	（形）	consistent
10. 基础	jīchǔ	（名）	basis
11. 语音	yǔyīn	（名）	speech sound
12. 标准	biāozhǔn	（名、形）	standard; standard
13. 词汇	cíhuì	（名）	vocabulary
14. 语法	yǔfǎ	（名）	grammar
15. 系统	xìtǒng	（名）	system
16. 程度	chéngdù	（名）	degree
17. 推广	tuīguǎng	（动）	popularize
18. 以	yǐ	（动、介、连）	take... as; by; so as

Chinese Crash Course

19. 交际	jiāojì	（动）	communicate
20. 致力	zhìlì	（动）	dedicate
21. 统一	tǒngyī	（动、形）	unify; unified
22. 加强	jiāqiáng	（动）	strengthen
23. 发挥	fāhuī	（动）	play

专有名词　Proper Nouns

1. 北方方言	Běifāng fāngyán	North dialect
2. 吴方言	Wú fāngyán	Wu dialect
3. 湘方言	Xiāng fāngyán	Xiang dialect
4. 赣方言	Gàn fāngyán	Gan dialect
5. 客家方言	Kèjiā fāngyán	Hakka dialect
6. 闽方言	Mǐn fāngyán	Min dialect
7. 粤方言	Yuè fāngyán	Yue dialect

Lesson Fifteen Putonghua and dialects

 句 型 Sentence Patterns

1. 不可避免地……

学习汉语的普通话，不可避免地要接触到各地方言。

It is inevitable to bring you into contact with many dialects when you learn *Putonghua*.

大家在学习外语的过程中不可避免地要遇到很多困难。

It is inevitable (unavoidable) to meet many difficulties in the course of learning foreign languages.

2. 分为……

现代汉语可以分为七大方言区。

Modern Chinese can be divided into seven dialect districts.

中国的地域文化可以简单地分为北方文化和南方文化。

The Chinese regional culture can be simply divided into northern culture and southern culture.

3. 以……为……

北方方言以北京话为代表。

Beijing accent is the representative of the North dialects.

普通话以北方方言为基础，以北京语音为标准音。

Putonghua is based on the North dialects and takes the Beijing accent as the standard pronunciation.

4. 致力于……

几十年来中国一直致力于推广普通话。

The government has been dedicated to popularize *Putonghua* for dozens of years.

他一生都致力于教育事业。

He is dedicated to the cause of education all his life.

注 释 Annotations

1. 与　*yǔ*

"与"做介词或连词多用于书面语。例如：

"Yǔ" as a preposition or conjunction is mostly used in written Chinese. For example:

他的专业与文学有关。

His major is related to literature.

每次与你相见，都让我惊奇。

Each time I meet you, I am surprised.

我的父亲与母亲二十年前就生活在这里。

My father and mother lived here twenty years ago.

他们是如此地激动与兴奋。

They are so excited and moved.

他们的神情与声音深深地打动了我。

Their expressions and voices moved me deeply.

Lesson Fifteen Putonghua and dialects

2. 以　　yǐ

"以……为"相当于"把……作为……"或"认为……是……",这里的"以"是动词。例如:

"Yǐ……wéi" equals "bǎ……zuòwéi……" or "rènwéi……shì……". "Yǐ" is a verb here. For example:

这个活动以留学生为主。

This activity is mainly for the overseas students.

我们不能以考试成绩为评价学生的标准。

We can't judge a student by his test results.

"以"做连词时表示目的。例如:

When "yǐ" is used as a conjunction, it means purpose. For example:

我们推广普通话,以使社会交际变得方便。

We popularize *Putonghua* to make social communication more convenient.

我们要进行政治、经济、文化等各方面的交流,以加强双方的了解与合作。

We make political, economic and cultural exchanges to strengthen our mutual understanding and cooperation.

我们反复讨论以找到最好的解决方式。

We discussed repeatedly in order to find out the best solution.

Chinese Crash Course

练 习　Exercises

一 根据课文完成词语搭配　Complete the following word-collocations according to the text.

接触(　　　)　　　(　　)的分歧　　　历史(　　)

复杂的(　　)　　　重视(　　　)　　　推广(　　)

民族(　　　)　　　发挥(　　　)　　　社会(　　)

二 选择填空　Choose the correct answers.

1. 我们决定改变计划(　　)避免更大的损失。

　A 而　　　　B 而且　　　C 以　　　D 为

2. 北方方言以北京话(　　)代表。

　A 被　　　　B 为　　　　C 于　　　D 是

3. 当地政府一直(　　　)经济发展。

　A 为了　　　B 推广　　　C 加强　　　D 致力于

三 模仿句型造句　Make sentences with the given words and sentence patterns.

1. 以……为……

2. 不可避免地……

3. 分为……

Lesson Fifteen　Putonghua and dialects

四　选词填空　Fill in the following blanks with the proper words.

基础　　一致　　避免　　标准　　广泛

1. 我们应该(　　)事故的发生。
2. 北方方言是中国使用最(　　)的一种方言。
3. 我们要重视并加强(　　)教育。
4. 在会上,大家的意见很(　　)。
5. 你的发音真(　　)!

相关阅读
Related Reading

(一)

　　Zhōnghuá Rénmín Gònghéguó shì tǒngyī de duōmínzú
　　中　华　人　民　共　和　国　是　统一　的　多　民　族
guójiā. Qìjīn wéizhǐ, zhōngyāng zhèngfǔ quèrèn de
国　家。迄　今　为　止,中　央　政　府　确　认　的
mínzú gòng wǔshíliù ge, yǒu Hàn、Měnggǔ、Huí、Zàng、Wéiwú'ěr、
民　族　共　56　个,有　汉、蒙　古、回、藏、维　吾　尔、
Miáo、Yí、Zhuàng、Bùyī、Cháoxiān、Mǎn、Dòng、Yáo、Bái、Tǔjiā、
苗、彝、壮、布　依、朝　鲜、满、侗、瑶、白、土　家、
Hāní、Hāsàkè、Dǎi děng. Zhè wǔshíliù ge mínzú jiù xiàng
哈　尼、哈　萨　克、傣　等。这　56　个　民　族　就　像
wǔshíliù duǒ huā, zài Zhōngguó de dàdì shang kāifàng zhe.
56　　朵　花,在　中　国　的　大　地　上　开　放　着。
　　Mùqián, Zhōngguó wǔshíwǔ ge shǎoshù mínzú zhōng, chú Huí-
　　目　前,中　国　55　个　少　数　民　族　中,除　回
zú hé Mǎnzú tōngyòng Hànyǔ zhī wài, qíyú wǔshísān ge
族　和　满　族　通　用　汉　语　之　外,其　余　53　个

民族都有自己的民族语言。有文字的民族有21个，共使用27种文字，其中13种文字是由政府帮助创制或改进的。

在长期的统一过程中，经济、文化交往把中国各民族紧密地联系在一起，从而形成了相互依存、相互促进、共同发展的关系，创造和发展了中华文明。中国各民族相互依存的政治、经济、文化联系，使其在长期的历史发展中有着共同的命运和共同的利益，产生了牢固的亲和力、凝聚力。

根据阅读内容判断正误：

1. 中国所有的民族都有自己的语言。　　　　（　）
2. 大多数少数民族有自己的文字。　　　　　（　）
3. 中国56个民族的团结是有历史原因的。　　（　）

Lesson Fifteen Putonghua and dialects

（二）

南腔北调、各说各话，曾让多少中国人无法交流；九州共语、四海同音，更是几代中国人的愿望。为了推广普通话，促进文化交流、经济发展，增强中华民族的凝聚力，由全国推广普通话宣传周领导小组办公室主办，北京今日育民文化传播有限公司承办的推广普通话形象大使选拔赛将于2005年9月29日在北京正式启动；随后，全国各省、市、自治区也将陆续启动。

1956年2月6日，国务院发布了《关于推广普通话的指示》，到现在已经将近50年。在这50年里，推广

普通话工作取得了长足的进展,普通话在全国各地的普及程度越来越高;但同社会发展的紧迫需要相比,实现全国普及普通话的工作仍然任重而道远,需要千千万万个推广普通话志愿者和全民的共同努力。

本次大赛由中央电视台著名主持人王小丫担任公益宣传形象大使,许多演艺界、文化界,甚至工商界的名流都参加了大赛宣传片的制作,他们以真诚、幽默的语言,各不相同的视角,畅谈了自己对推广普通话重要性的看法。

根据阅读内容判断正误:

1. 中国政府推广普通话的工作是在改革开放后才开始的。(　　)
2. 中国现在的普通话普及程度越来越高。(　　)
3. 普通话大赛是在主持人之间进行的。(　　)

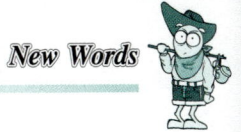

生 词
New Words

A

爱国	ài//guó	（动）	love one's country	L5
安静	ānjìng	（动、形）	quiet; noiseless	L8

B

把握	bǎwò	（动）	hold	L10
白头偕老	báitóu xié lǎo		live to old age in conjugal bliss	L4
百看不厌	bǎi kàn bú yàn		be worth watching a hundred times	L2
包含	bāohán	（动）	include	L2
宝贝	bǎobèi	（名）	baby	L10
保佑	bǎoyòu	（动）	bless	L12
北方人	běifāngrén	（名）	northerner	L13
背面	bèimiàn	（名）	back	L12
比喻	bǐyù	（名、动）	metaphor; liken to	L8
必要	bìyào	（形）	necessary	L9
避免	bìmiǎn	（动）	avoid	L15

Chinese Crash Course

便	biàn	(副)	so	L13
遍	biàn	(量)	(*measure word*) time	L2
标准	biāozhǔn	(名、形)	standard; standard	L15
表明	biǎomíng	(动)	indicate	L7
表现	biǎoxiàn	(动、名)	represent; representation	L4
并	bìng	(副)	together	L3
不断	búduàn	(副)	constantly	L14
不过	búguò	(连)	but	L1
补充	bǔchōng	(动)	complement	L13
部分	bùfen	(名)	part	L2

才子佳人	cáizǐ jiārén		talented scholars and beautiful ladies	L4
差异	chāyì	(名)	difference, disparity	L13
长期	chángqī	(名)	long term	L13
唱词	chàngcí	(名)	libretto	L6
超过	chāoguò	(动)	exceed	L1
沉默	chénmò	(形)	silent	L11
成立	chénglì	(动)	found	L4
成人	chéngrén	(名)	adult	L2
成熟	chéngshú	(形)	mature	L6
成语	chéngyǔ	(名)	idiom	L4
诚实	chéngshí	(形)	honest	L5

New Words

程度	chéngdù	（名）	degree	L15
吃惊	chī//jīng	（动）	surprise	L8
吃苦	chī//kǔ	（动）	bear hardships	L5
持续	chíxù	（动）	continue	L1
充满	chōngmǎn	（动）	fill	L10
出入境	chū-rùjìng		entry and exit	L14
触动	chùdòng	（动）	touch	L11
创造	chuàngzào	（动）	create	L14
纯洁	chúnjié	（形）	pure	L4
词汇	cíhuì	（名）	vocabulary	L15
此	cǐ	（代）	this	L3
从前	cóngqián	（名）	once upon a time	L9
促进	cùjìn	（动）	facilitate	L14
存在	cúnzài	（动）	exist	L1
措施	cuòshī	（名）	measure	L14

D

打动	dǎdòng	（动）	move	L11
打工	dǎ//gōng	（动）	do a temporary job	L13
大量	dàliàng	（形）	abundant	L13
大陆	dàlù	（名）	mainland of China	L14
代替	dàitì	（动）	take the place of	L10
担忧	dānyōu	（动）	worry	L9
胆子	dǎnzi	（名）	courage	L9

Chinese Crash Course

倒	dào	(动)	reverse	L11
道德	dàodé	(名)	moral	L2
道家	Dàojiā	(名)	Taoist	L2
得到	dédào	(动)	get	L6
等	děng	(助)	etc.	L3
地理	dìlǐ	(名)	geography	L7
地球	dìqiú	(名)	earth	L9
动情	dòng//qíng	(动)	become excited	L11
读	dú	(动)	read	L2
度过	dùguò	(动)	spend	L3
短浅	duǎnqiǎn	(形)	shortsighted	L8
蹲	dūn	(动)	squat	L8
多么	duōme	(副)	how	L7
躲藏	duǒcáng	(动)	hide	L9

E

而	ér	(连)	but	L2

F

发表	fābiǎo	(动)	publish	L14
发愁	fā//chóu	(动)	be anxious	L9
发达	fādá	(形)	developed	L7
发挥	fāhuī	(动)	play	L15

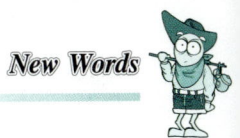

New Words

法定	fǎdìng	(形)	legal	L3
法律	fǎlǜ	(名)	law	L2
翻	fān	(动)	look for	L12
烦恼	fánnǎo	(形)	vexed	L9
繁荣	fánróng	(形、动)	prosperous; flourish	L6
范围	fànwéi	(名)	scope	L1
方块字	fāngkuàizì	(名)	(square-shaped) Chinese character	L1
方言	fāngyán	(名)	dialect	L15
房地产	fángdìchǎn	(名)	real estate	L3
放宽	fàngkuān	(动)	relax	L14
放松	fàngsōng	(动)	relax	L3
分布	fēnbù	(动)	distribute	L15
分歧	fēnqí	(名)	difference	L15
氛围	fēnwéi	(名)	atmosphere	L6
风景	fēngjǐng	(名)	scenery	L5
封	fēng	(量)	*measure word*	L10
抚摸	fǔmō	(动)	touch	L10
负担	fùdān	(动、名)	shoulder; burden	L13
复杂	fùzá	(形)	complicated	L2

G

改革	gǎigé	(动)	reform	L4
赶上	gǎnshang	(动)	catch up with	L3

Chinese Crash Course

敢	gǎn	(助动)	dare	L12
感觉	gǎnjué	(名、动)	feeling; feel	L10
感叹	gǎntàn	(动)	sigh with feeling	L11
港口	gǎngkǒu	(名)	port	L7
高雅	gāoyǎ	(形)	elegant	L5
隔	gé	(动)	separate	L10
根	gēn	(名)	root	L7
根本	gēnběn	(名、副)	root; at all	L8
根据	gēnjù	(介)	according to	L9
工人	gōngrén	(名)	worker	L4
公民	gōngmín	(名)	citizen	L5
构成	gòuchéng	(动)	constitute	L2
鼓励	gǔlì	(动)	encourage	L6
鼓掌	gǔ//zhǎng	(动)	applaud	L6
故乡	gùxiāng	(名)	hometown	L2
关键	guānjiàn	(形、名)	crucial; key	L5
关注	guānzhù	(动)	pay close attention to	L6
观念	guānniàn	(名)	concept	L3
观众	guānzhòng	(名)	audience	L6
官员	guānyuán	(名)	official	L1
广大	guǎngdà	(形)	immense	L8
广泛	guǎngfàn	(形)	wide	L15
跪	guì	(动)	kneel down	L12
国庆	guóqìng	(名)	National Day	L3
过程	guòchéng	(名)	process	L4

New Words

H

孩子	háizi	(名)	child	L2
海龟	hǎiguī	(名)	sea turtle, marine turtle	L8
海外	hǎiwài	(名)	overseas	L1
海洋	hǎiyáng	(名)	sea	L7
喊	hǎn	(动)	shout	L6
好奇	hàoqí	(形)	curious	L12
好奇心	hàoqíxīn	(名)	curiosity	L12
何必	hébì	(副)	there is no need	L9
河	hé	(名)	river	L8
河流	héliú	(名)	river	L8
盒子	hézi	(名)	box	L12
厚	hòu	(形)	thick	L12
户口	hùkǒu	(名)	registered permanent residence	L13
华人	huárén	(名)	overseas Chinese	L7
怀念	huáiniàn	(动)	miss	L12
黄金	huángjīn	(名)	gold	L3
婚姻	hūnyīn	(名)	marriage	L4
活力	huólì	(名)	energy	L13
活跃	huóyuè	(动、形)	activate; brisk	L13

J

几乎	jīhū	(副)	nearly	L9
积极	jījí	(形)	active	L4
基础	jīchǔ	(名)	basis	L15
即使	jíshǐ	(连)	even if	L8
记忆	jìyì	(名)	memory	L12
记者	jìzhě	(名)	reporter	L14
纪录	jìlù	(名)	record	L14
继承	jìchéng	(动)	inherit	L6
加强	jiāqiáng	(动)	strengthen	L15
夹带	jiādài	(动)	carry with	L11
假如	jiǎrú	(连)	if	L9
价值	jiàzhí	(名)	value	L3
假日	jiàrì	(名)	holiday	L3
嫁	jià	(动)	marry	L4
简化	jiǎnhuà	(动)	simplify	L14
见识	jiànshi	(名)	insight	L8
健康	jiànkāng	(名、形)	health; healthy	L3
讲	jiǎng	(动)	tell	L2
讲究	jiǎngjiu	(动、形)	pay attention to; tasteful	L5
交际	jiāojì	(动)	communicate	L15
交流	jiāoliú	(动)	communicate	L13
交通	jiāotōng	(名)	traffic	L3
焦点	jiāodiǎn	(名)	focus	L3

New Words

角度	jiǎodù	(名)	angle	L7
狡猾	jiǎohuá	(形)	cunning	L5
教育	jiàoyù	(名)	education	L14
街道	jiēdào	(名)	street	L1
节/节日	jié/jiérì	(名)	festival	L3
禁不住	jīnbuzhù	(动)	cannot help	L12
进入	jìnrù	(动)	enter	L13
经商	jīng//shāng	(动)	do business	L7
惊奇	jīngqí	(动)	surprise	L10
惊人	jīngrén	(形)	surprising	L13
精神	jīngshén	(名)	spirit	L2
井	jǐng	(名)	well	L8
井底之蛙	jǐng dǐ zhī wā		a frog in a well	L8
旧	jiù	(形)	old	L12
居民	jūmín	(名)	resident	L3
巨大	jùdà	(形)	huge	L7
据	jù	(介)	according to	L1
军人	jūnrén	(名)	soldier	L4

K

卡拉OK	kǎlā-OK		karaoke	L11
开放	kāifàng	(动、形)	open; open	L4
开玩笑	kāi wánxiào		make a joke	L4
科学	kēxué	(名)	science	L14

Chinese Crash Course

棵	kē	（量）	measure word	L7
可爱	kě'ài	（形）	lovely	L10
可怕	kěpà	（形）	fearful	L10
肯	kěn	（动）	be willing to	L6
控制	kòngzhì	（动）	control	L7
快速	kuàisù	（形）	quick	L1
扩大	kuòdà	（动）	expand	L14

L

辣椒	làjiāo	（名）	pepper	L5
来往	láiwǎng	（动）	come and leave	L14
懒惰	lǎnduò	（形）	lazy	L5
郎才女貌	láng cái nǚ mào		man has ability and woman has good looks	L4
浪漫	làngmàn	（形）	romantic	L4
劳动	láodòng	（动）	labor	L3
老大爷	lǎodàye	（名）	(honorific) old man	L11
老实	lǎoshi	（形）	honest	L5
老太太	lǎotàitai	（名）	old lady	L11
泪	lèi	（名）	tear	L11
离婚	lí//hūn	（动）	divorce	L4
礼貌	lǐmào	（名、形）	civility; polite	L5
理想	lǐxiǎng	（名、形）	ideal; ideal	L2
厉害	lìhai	（形）	stern	L5

New Words

立刻	lìkè	(副)	immediately	L6
利用	lìyòng	(动)	use	L3
例如	lìrú	(动)	take for example	L8
脸	liǎn	(名)	face	L10
脸谱	liǎnpǔ	(名)	facial makeup	L6
粮食	liángshi	(名)	food, grain	L13
两岸	liǎng'àn	(名)	both sides across the Taiwan Straits	L14
临	lín	(介)	about to	L12
领域	lǐngyù	(名)	field	L14
留言	liúyán	(名)	message	L12
流	liú	(动)	flow	L8
流动	liúdòng	(动)	flow	L13
录取	lùqǔ	(动)	enroll	L12
路牌	lùpái	(名)	street nameplate	L1
率	lǜ	(名)	rate	L4
乱	luàn	(形)	disorderly	L13

M

门当户对	mén dāng hù duì		be well-matched in social status	L4
梦	mèng	(名)	dream	L10
秘密	mìmì	(名)	secret	L7
面子	miànzi	(名)	reputation	L13

Chinese Crash Course

民族	mínzú	（名）	nation, ethnic group	L6
明显	míngxiǎn	（形）	distinct	L13
莫名其妙	mò míng qí miào		without rhyme or reason	L9
某	mǒu	（代）	some	L11
墓	mù	（名）	tomb, grave	L12

N

南方人	nánfāngrén	（名）	southerner	L13
内	nèi	（名）	inside	L1
内部	nèibù	（名）	interior	L15
能干	nénggàn	（形）	capable, competent	L5
泥	ní	（名）	mud	L8
年纪	niánjì	（名）	age	L11
农民	nóngmín	（名）	farmer	L13

P

怕	pà	（动）	fear	L5
泡	pào	（动）	soak	L8
陪	péi	（动）	accompany	L11
碰	pèng	（动）	meet	L8
屁股	pìgu	（名）	ass	L11
片面	piànmiàn	（形）	one-sided	L5
票友	piàoyǒu	（名）	amateur performer	L6

New Words

品德	pǐndé	(名)	moral character	L4
平安	píng'ān	(形)	safe	L12
平等	píngděng	(形)	equal	L4
平衡	pínghéng	(形)	balanced	L13
破坏	pòhuài	(动)	destroy	L12
朴实	pǔshí	(形)	plain	L7
普通话	pǔtōnghuà	(名)	*Putonghua* (standard Chinese)	L15

妻子	qīzi	(名)	wife	L12
期限	qīxiàn	(名)	time limit	L14
其次	qícì	(代)	secondly	L13
其实	qíshí	(副)	as a matter of fact	L5
其中	qízhōng	(名)	within	L1
奇怪	qíguài	(形)	strange	L9
杞人忧天	Qǐ rén yōu tiān		like the man of Qi who feared that the sky might fall	L9
浅	qiǎn	(形)	shallow	L8
强	qiáng	(形)	strong	L7
悄悄	qiāoqiāo	(副)	quietly	L12
亲爱	qīn'ài	(形)	dear	L10
亲爱的	qīn'ài de		darling	L10
亲热	qīnrè	(形)	intimate	L12

勤劳	qínláo	(形)	industrious	L5
青蛙	qīngwā	(名)	frog	L8
清晨	qīngchén	(名)	early morning	L11
情感	qínggǎn	(名)	emotion	L4
情歌	qínggē	(名)	love song	L11
情节	qíngjié	(名)	plot	L2
情书	qíngshū	(名)	love letter	L10
圈子	quānzi	(名)	circle	L7
劝	quàn	(动)	persuade	L9
缺少	quēshǎo	(动)	lack	L6

R

热闹	rènao	(形)	lively	L11
热情	rèqíng	(形)	enthusiastic	L6
人才	réncái	(名)	talented people	L13
人次	réncì	(量)	(measure word) person-time	L14
人家	rénjia	(代)	others	L9
人口	rénkǒu	(名)	population	L13
人生	rénshēng	(名)	life	L2
忍	rěn	(动)	endure	L12
仍然	réngrán	(副)	still	L9
如此	rúcǐ	(代)	so	L11
如今	rújīn	(名)	now	L6
儒家	Rújiā	(名)	Confucianist	L2
入出境	rù-chūjìng		exit and entry	L14

S

散步	sàn//bù	（动）	take a walk	L8
沙哑	shāyǎ	（形）	husky	L11
山	shān	（名）	hill	L7
善于	shànyú	（动）	be good at	L13
舍不得	shěbude	（动）	hate to part with	L12
申请	shēnqǐng	（动）	apply	L14
深度	shēndù	（名）	depth	L8
神情	shénqíng	（名）	expression	L11
升温	shēngwēn	（动）	increase in temperature	L1
生命	shēngmìng	（名）	life	L2
生命力	shēngmìnglì	（名）	vitality	L6
生意	shēngyi	（名）	business	L5
声音	shēngyīn	（名）	sound	L10
失败	shībài	（动）	fail	L5
失去	shīqù	（动）	lose	L10
石头	shítou	（名）	stone	L11
时常	shícháng	（副）	frequently	L12
时尚	shíshàng	（名、形）	fashion; fashionable	L1
实际	shíjì	（形、名）	practical; reality	L9
实力	shílì	（名）	strength	L7
实施	shíshī	（动）	put into effect	L14
食宿	shí sù		board and lodging	L3
市场经济	shìchǎng jīngjì		market economy	L13

Chinese Crash Course

世纪	shìjì	（名）	century	L7
手续	shǒuxù	（名）	procedure	L14
首	shǒu		first	L1
首届	shǒujiè	（数量）	first session	L1
首先	shǒuxiān	（副、连）	first; first of all	L13
书房	shūfáng	（名）	study	L12
属于	shǔyú	（动）	belong to	L1
树	shù	（名）	tree	L7
树根	shùgēn	（名）	root of a tree	L7
数字	shùzì	（名）	number	L7
说法	shuōfa	（名）	saying	L5
思念	sīniàn	（动）	miss	L10
思想	sīxiǎng	（名）	thinking	L2
随	suí	（动）	follow	L12
随即	suíjí	（副）	immediately	L11
随着	suí zhe		with	L12
缩小	suōxiǎo	（动）	reduce	L13

塌	tā	（动）	collapse	L9
太阳	tàiyáng	（名）	sun	L11
探亲	tàn//qīn	（动）	go home and visit one's family	L14
特有	tè yǒu		unique	L6

New Words

特征	tèzhēng	（名）	characteristic	L7
提供	tígōng	（动）	provide	L13
体会	tǐhuì	（动）	experience	L10
体育	tǐyù	（名）	sports	L14
天空	tiānkōng	（名）	sky	L9
天使	tiānshǐ	（名）	angel	L10
跳	tiào	（动）	jump	L8
跳舞	tiào//wǔ	（动）	dance	L11
同居	tóngjū	（动）	cohabit	L4
童话	tónghuà	（名）	fairy tale	L2
统计	tǒngjì	（动）	statistics	L1
统一	tǒngyī	（动、形）	unify; unified	L15
痛苦	tòngkǔ	（形）	painful	L10
投入	tóurù	（动、形）	devote; devoted	L11
团结	tuánjié	（动、形）	unite; united	L7
团聚	tuánjù	（动）	unite	L3
推广	tuīguǎng	（动）	popularize	L15
退场	tuì//chǎng	（动）	leave	L6

外星人	wàixīngrén	（名）	extraterrestrial being	L9
玩笑	wánxiào	（名）	joke	L4
网页	wǎngyè	（名）	webpage	L1
网站	wǎngzhàn	（名）	website	L1

危机	wēijī	(名)	crisis	L6
微笑	wēixiào	(动)	smile	L10
唯一	wéiyī	(形)	only	L3
温和	wēnhé	(形)	gentle	L5
温柔	wēnróu	(形)	gentle and soft	L10
吻	wěn	(名、动)	kiss; kiss	L10
无论	wúlùn	(连)	no matter what	L9
武	wǔ		martial arts	L2
武侠	wǔxiá	(名)	chivalrous swordsman	L2

X

戏剧	xìjù	(名)	drama, theater	L6
戏剧家	xìjùjiā	(名)	dramatist	L6
戏迷	xìmí	(名)	theater fan	L6
戏曲艺术	xìqǔ yìshù		drama	L6
系统	xìtǒng	(名)	system	L15
侠	xiá		chivalrous man	L2
鲜艳	xiānyàn	(形)	bright-colored	L6
现代	xiàndài	(名、形)	modern times; modern	L7
现实	xiànshí	(名、形)	reality; realistic	L4
现象	xiànxiàng	(名)	phenomenon	L2
限制	xiànzhì	(动)	confine	L8
献出	xiànchū	(动)	sacrifice	L2

New Words

相敬如宾	xiāng jìng rú bīn		respect each other as if the other were a guest	L4
相似	xiāngsì	(形)	similar	L2
想象	xiǎngxiàng	(名、动)	imagination; imagine	L7
小气	xiǎoqi	(形)	stingy	L5
小说	xiǎoshuō	(名)	novel	L2
小心	xiǎoxīn	(动、形)	be careful; careful	L5
心	xīn	(名)	heart	L10
欣赏	xīnshǎng	(动)	enjoy	L6
新闻	xīnwén	(名)	news	L14
信用	xìnyòng	(名)	credit	L5
行为	xíngwéi	(名)	behavior	L2
形成	xíngchéng	(动)	become	L2
许多	xǔduō	(形)	many	L6
选修	xuǎnxiū	(动)	take as an elective (course)	L1

压	yā	(动)	press	L9
延长	yáncháng	(动)	extend	L3
研究生	yánjiūshēng	(名)	graduate student	L12
眼光	yǎnguāng	(名)	vision	L8
眼前	yǎnqián	(名)	at present	L10
遥远	yáoyuǎn	(形)	far	L10

钥匙	yàoshi	（名）	key	L12
野蛮	yěmán	（形）	wild	L5
医疗	yīliáo	（名）	medical treatment	L14
一共	yígòng	（副）	altogether	L3
一致	yízhì	（形）	consistent	L15
以	yǐ	（动、介、连）	take...as; by; so as	L15
以及	yǐjí	（连）	as well as	L14
亿	yì	（数）	a hundred million	L7
义气	yìqì	（名、形）	personal loyalty; chivalrous	L5
意义	yìyì	（名）	meaning	L3
引起	yǐnqǐ	（动）	arouse	L6
引申	yǐnshēn	（动）	extend	L9
隐藏	yǐncáng	（动）	hide	L11
永远	yǒngyuǎn	（形）	forever	L10
勇敢	yǒnggǎn	（形）	brave	L2
优点	yōudiǎn	（名）	advantage	L13
忧愁	yōuchóu	（形）	worried	L9
由	yóu	（介）	from	L14
犹豫	yóuyù	（动）	hesitate	L12
有趣	yǒuqù	（形）	interesting	L2
有时	yǒushí	（副）	sometimes	L8
有时候	yǒushíhou	（副）	sometimes	L3
有效	yǒuxiào	（形）	valid	L14
有意义	yǒu yìyì		meaningful	L3

New Words

于	yú	（介）	at	L10
语法	yǔfǎ	（名）	grammar	L15
语音	yǔyīn	（名）	speech sound	L15
原因	yuányīn	（名）	reason	L9
约/大约	yuē/dàyuē	（副）	about	L1
云	yún	（名）	cloud	L7

Z

再说	zàishuō	（连）	what is more	L9
脏	zāng	（形）	dirty	L13
占	zhàn	（动）	account for	L1
障碍	zhàng'ài	（名）	impediment	L1
召开	zhàokāi	（动）	hold	L1
照	zhào	（动）	shine	L11
真诚	zhēnchéng	（形）	sincere	L10
真情	zhēnqíng	（名）	true feeling	L11
真心	zhēnxīn	（名）	sincerity	L10
真正	zhēnzhèng	（形、副）	real; really	L6
整洁	zhěngjié	（形）	tidy	L5
正式	zhèngshì	（形）	formal	L14
正义	zhèngyì	（名）	justice	L2
政治	zhèngzhì	（名）	politics	L4
……之一	……zhī yī		one of...	L4
只	zhī	（量）	*measure word*	L8

知识	zhīshi	(名)	knowledge	L5
纸	zhǐ	(名)	paper	L12
至	zhì	(动)	to	L1
制度	zhìdù	(名)	system	L13
致力	zhìlì	(动)	dedicate	L15
种类	zhǒnglèi	(名)	kind	L6
众多	zhòngduō	(形)	numerous	L15
逐渐	zhújiàn	(副)	gradually	L14
主人	zhǔrén	(名)	owner	L8
专门	zhuānmén	(形)	special	L6
专注	zhuānzhù	(形)	absorbed	L11
准确	zhǔnquè	(形)	exact	L7
资产	zīchǎn	(名)	property, assets	L7
自言自语	zì yán zì yǔ		speak to oneself	L9
自由自在	zìyóu zìzài		free	L8
总	zǒng	(副)	always	L12
总算	zǒngsuàn	(副)	eventually	L10
遵守	zūnshǒu	(动)	obey	L5
作为	zuòwéi	(动)	act as	L1
作用	zuòyòng	(名)	effect	L13

专有名词
Proper Nouns

安徽	Ānhuī	Anhui (Province)	L5
北方方言	Běifāng fāngyán	North dialect	L15
出入境管理局	Chū-rùjìng Guǎnlǐ Jú	Entry and Exit Administration Bureau	L14
春节	Chūn Jié	Spring Festival	L3
德国	Déguó	Germany	L1
德语	Déyǔ	German	L1
东北	Dōngběi	Northeast	L5
东南亚	Dōngnányà	Southeast Asia	L7
法语	Fǎyǔ	French	L1
福建	Fújiàn	Fujian (Province)	L7
赣方言	Gàn fāngyán	Gan dialect	L15
公安部	Gōng'ān Bù	Ministry of Public Security	L14
广东	Guǎngdōng	Guangdong (Province)	L5
韩国	Hánguó	South Korea	L1
汉堡市	Hànbǎo Shì	Hamburg (City)	L1
湖北	Húběi	Hubei (Province)	L5
客家方言	Kèjiā fāngyán	Hakka dialect	L15
马可·波罗	Mǎkě·Bōluó	Marco Polo	L7
闽方言	Mǐn fāngyán	Min dialect	L15

南宋	Nánsòng	Southern Song Dynasty	L7
泉州	Quánzhōu	Quanzhou (City)	L7
山西	Shānxī	Shanxi (Province)	L5
十一国庆节	Shí-Yī Guóqìng Jié	National Day of October First	L3
台湾	Táiwān	Taiwan (Province)	L14
泰国	Tàiguó	Thailand	L1
吴方言	Wú fāngyán	Wu dialect	L15
五一国际劳动节	Wǔ-Yī Guójì Láodòng Jié	May Day	L3
西北	Xīběi	Northwest	L5
湘方言	Xiāng fāngyán	Xiang dialect	L15
意大利	Yìdàlì	Italy	L7
印度尼西亚	Yìndùníxīyà	Indonesia	L7
粤方言	Yuè fāngyán	Yue dialect	L15
浙江	Zhèjiāng	Zhejiang (Province)	L5
中秋节	Zhōngqiū Jié	Mid-Autumn Festival	L3

Appendix 1

Táng Shī Wǔ Shǒu
唐 诗 五 首

Five poems of the Tang Dynasty

Jìng Yè Sī
静 夜 思

Lǐ Bái
李 白

Chuáng qián míng yuè guāng,
床　　前　　明　　月　　光，

Yí shì dì shang shuāng.
疑　　是　　地　　上　　霜。

Jǔ tóu wàng míng yuè,
举　　头　　望　　明　　月，

Dī tóu sī gù xiāng.
低　　头　　思　　故　　乡。

In the Quiet Night

So bright a gleam on the foot of my bed.
Could there have been a frost already?
Lifting myself to look, I found that it was moonlight.
Sinking back again, I thought suddenly of my home.

Wàng Lú Shān Pùbù
望 庐 山 瀑 布

Lǐ Bái
李 白

Rì	zhào	xiāng	lú	shēng	zǐ	yān,
日	照	香	炉	生	紫	烟，
Yáo	kàn	pù	bù	guà	qián	chuān.
遥	看	瀑	布	挂	前	川。
Fēi	liú	zhí	xià	sān	qiān	chǐ,
飞	流	直	下	三	千	尺，
Yí	shì	yín	hé	luò	jiǔ	tiān.
疑	是	银	河	落	九	天。

Watching the Waterfall at Mt. Lushan

Violet smoke rises from Censer Peak in the sunlight.
Like an upended stream the fall hangs there.
Its torrent dashes down three thousand feet from up.
I wonder if the Milky Way from the Ninth Sky is falling down to the earth.

Appendix 1

Qīngmíng
清 明

Dù Mù
杜 牧

Qīng	míng	shí	jié	yǔ	fēn	fēn,
清	明	时	节	雨	纷	纷，
Lù	shang	xíng	rén	yù	duàn	hún.
路	上	行	人	欲	断	魂。
Jiè	wèn	jiǔ	jiā	hé	chù	yǒu?
借	问	酒	家	何	处	有？
Mù	tóng	yáo	zhǐ	Xìng	huā	cūn.
牧	童	遥	指	杏	花	村。

Qingming

It drizzles endlessly during Qingming[1] period.

Travelers along the road look gloomy and miserable.

When I ask a shepherd boy where I can find a tavern.

He points at a distant hamlet nestling amidst apricot blossoms.

---

[1] Qingming is one of the twenty four solar terms falling on the 5th or 6th of April. On this day people go grave-sweeping to honor the memory of the dead.

Dēng Guànquè Lóu
登 鹳 雀 楼

Wáng Zhīhuàn
王 之 涣

Bái	rì	yī	shān	jìn,
白	日	依	山	尽,
Huáng	Hé	rù	hǎi	liú.
黄	河	入	海	流。
Yù	qióng	qiān	lǐ	mù,
欲	穷	千	里	目,
Gèng	shàng	yì	céng	lóu.
更	上	一	层	楼。

Mounting the Stork Tower

The white sun sets behind the mountain.
The Yellow River flows into the sea.
Go further up one flight of stairs.
And you will widen your view one thousand *li*.
(Translated by Gu Hongming)

Appendix 1

Jiāng Xuě
江 雪

Liǔ Zōngyuán
柳 宗 元

Qiān	shān	niǎo	fēi	jué,
千	山	鸟	飞	绝，
Wàn	jìng	rén	zōng	miè.
万	径	人	踪	灭。
Gū	zhōu	suō	lì	wēng,
孤	舟	蓑	笠	翁，
Dú	diào	hán	jiāng	xuě.
独	钓	寒	江	雪。

River Snow

A hundred mountains with no bird in sight.
A thousand paths without a footprint.
A little boat, a bamboo cloak.
An old man fishing in the cold river-snow.

Appendix 2

谚语八则
Yànyǔ Bā Zé

Eight proverbs

差之毫厘,失之千里
Chā zhī háolí, shī zhī qiānlǐ

虽然是极小的差错,却对结果造成了很大的影响。
Suīrán shì jí xiǎo de chācuò, què duì jiéguǒ zàochéngle hěn dà de yǐngxiǎng.

这条谚语告诉人们:做事要求精细准确,即使极小的差错,恐怕也会对结果造成重大的影响。
Zhè tiáo yànyǔ gàosu rénmen: zuò shì yāoqiú jīngxì zhǔnquè, jíshǐ jí xiǎo de chācuò, kǒngpà yě huì duì jiéguǒ zàochéng zhòngdà de yǐngxiǎng.

A little error may lead to a large discrepancy

An error of the breadth of a single hair can lead a thousand *li* astray.

This proverb tells us that whatever we do, we must be accurate, otherwise we may make serious mistakes.

道高一尺,魔高一丈
Dào gāo yì chǐ, mó gāo yí zhàng

高僧的道行增高一尺,恶魔的
Gāosēng de dàoheng zēnggāo yì chǐ, èmó de

Appendix 2

_{xiéqì   jiù   huì   suí   zhe   zēnggāo   yí   zhàng.}
邪 气 就 会 随 着 增 高 一 丈。
　　　　_{Zhè   tiáo   yànyǔ   gàosu   rénmen: Dàoheng   suīrán zēng-}
　　 这 条 谚 语 告 诉 人 们：道 行 虽 然 增
_{gāole   yì   chǐ,   dàn   shòu   èmó   de   yǐnyòu,   sàngshī}
高 了 一 尺，但 受 恶 魔 的 引 诱，丧 失
_{dàoheng   què   hěn   róngyì.   Yě   jiù   shì shuō   zuì'è   niàntou}
道 行 却 很 容 易。也 就 是 说 罪 恶 念 头
_{de   yǐnyòulì   gèng   dà.   Lìngwài   yě   zhǐ: Suīrán   zhèngyì}
的 引 诱 力 更 大。另 外 也 指：虽 然 正 义
_{de   shìqing   hěn   bu   róngyì   dédào   jiāqiáng,   dàn   xié'è}
的 事 情 很 不 容 易 得 到 加 强，但 邪 恶
_{zǒng huì xiǎngchū   bànfǎ   lái,   zhǎodào   kòngzi   zuān.   Yǐcǐ}
总 会 想 出 办 法 来，找 到 空 子 钻。以 此
_{gàojiè   wǒmen   yào   shíshí   dīfang   xié'è   de   dōngxi.}
告 诫 我 们 要 时 时 提 防 邪 恶 的 东 西。

As virtue rises one foot, evil rises ten

　　As the supernatural skill of a brilliant Buddist increases one foot, devil's power will increase ten times of it.

　　This proverb tells us that although the religious attainments of a Buddist increase, he faces more temptation and seduction from the devil. So it is easy for him to lose his attainments. It also indicates that righteous things are easy to strengthen, the devil always finds all kinds of ways to destroy them. So we should be on guard against it all the time.

_{Ěr   tīng   wéi   xū,   yǎn   jiàn   wéi   shí}
　　　　耳 听 为 虚，眼 见 为 实
_{Zhǐ   píng   ěrduo   tīngdào   de   wǎngwǎng shì xūjiǎ   de}
　　只 凭 耳 朵 听 到 的 往 往 是 虚 假 的

dōngxi, zhǐyǒu qīn yǎn kàndào de cái shì quèshí
东西，只有亲眼看到的才是确实
kěkào de.
可靠的。

Zhè tiáo yànyǔ gàosu rénmen: Chuánwén wǎngwǎng shì
这条谚语告诉人们：传闻往往是
bù kěkào de, zhǐyǒu qīn yǎn suǒ jiàn cái néng liǎojiě
不可靠的，只有亲眼所见才能了解
shìqing de zhēnxiàng. Suǒyǐ, duì rènhé shìqing dōu
事情的真相。所以，对任何事情都
bù kě qīngyì tīngxìn, ér shì yào yǐ shìshí zuòwéi
不可轻易听信，而是要以事实作为
yījù.
依据。

Seeing is believing

What is heard may be false but what is seen is true.

This proverb tells us that hearsay is often unreliable. Only when you see it by your own eyes can you know the truth. So do not trust any hearsay. The only thing you can believe is the fact.

Liúdé qīngshān zài, bú pà méi chái shāo
留得青山在，不怕没柴烧
Zhǐyào bǎ qīngshān liúzhù, jiù búyòng dānxīn méiyou
只要把青山留住，就不用担心没有
cháihuo shāo.
柴火烧。

Appendix 2

Zhè tiáo yànyǔ gàosu rénmen: Zhǐyào bǎocún shílì,
这 条 谚 语 告 诉 人 们：只 要 保 存 实 力，
nà jiù zǒng yǒu yì tiān kěyǐ huīfù guolai, yǒu lìliàng
那 就 总 有 一 天 可 以 恢 复 过 来，有 力 量
xiàng zuìzhōng mùbiāo qiánjìn.
向 最 终 目 标 前 进。

While there is life there is hope

As long as the green hills last, there'll always be wood to burn.

This proverb tells us that there will always be a day we can achieve our goal as long as we keep strength and faith.

Liángyào kǔ kǒu lì yú bìng, zhōngyán nì ěr lì yú xíng
良 药 苦 口 利 于 病，忠 言 逆 耳 利 于 行
Hǎo yào wèidao hěn kǔ, què yǒulì yú bìngqíng de
好 药 味 道 很 苦，却 有 利 于 病 情 的
hǎo zhuǎn; zhōngchéng de huà tīngzhe cì ěr, què yǒulì yú
好 转；忠 诚 的 话 听 着 刺 耳，却 有 利 于
rén de jìnbù.
人 的 进 步。
Zhè tiáo yànyǔ gàosu rénmen: Zhēnchéng de pīpíng
这 条 谚 语 告 诉 人 们：真 诚 的 批 评
hé quàngào jiù rútóng liángyào yíyàng, suīrán tīng qi-
和 劝 告 就 如 同 良 药 一 样，虽 然 听 起
lui bú shùn'ěr, dàn què duì zìjǐ yǒu suǒ bāngzhù,
来 不 顺 耳，但 却 对 自 己 有 所 帮 助，

Chinese Crash Course

shì　yǒulì　ér　wú　hài　de.
是 有 利 而 无 害 的。

Just as bitter medicine cures sickness, unpalatable advice benefits conduct

Good medicine tastes bitter, but it is beneficial to the health; honest advice may sound harsh, but it is beneficial to the people's development.

This proverb tells us that sincere criticism and advice are just the best medicine, although they sound unpleasant, they benefit your conduct.

Pǎole　héshang,　pǎo bu liǎomiào
跑 了 和 尚, 跑 不 了 庙

Héshang zhù zài miào li,　jíshǐ héshang táopǎole,
和 尚 住 在 庙 里, 即 使 和 尚 逃 跑 了,
miào háishi huì liú zài nàli.
庙 还 是 会 留 在 那 里。
Zhè zé yànyǔ shuōmíng: Yí ge rén táozǒule,
这 则 谚 语 说 明: 一 个 人 逃 走 了,
dàn tā de lǎocháo hái zài, zǒng yǒu yì tiān huì huílai,
但 他 的 老 巢 还 在, 总 有 一 天 会 回 来,
dào nà shí háishi huì bèi zhuāzhù, jiù shì shuō, jíshǐ
到 那 时 还 是 会 被 抓 住, 就 是 说, 即 使
dāngshí táopǎole, zuìzhōng háishi bù néng táotuō de.
当 时 逃 跑 了, 最 终 还 是 不 能 逃 脱 的。

Appendix 2

The monk may run away, but the temple can't run with him

The monk lives in the temple. Even though the monk escapes, the temple will still be there.

This proverb tells us that one may escape, but his house remains. He must be back some day, and he will be caught up then.

Rén bù kě mào xiàng, hǎishuǐ bù kě dǒu liáng
人 不 可 貌 相，海 水 不 可 斗 量

Hǎi li de shuǐ shì bù néng yòng dǒu lái cèliáng de,
海 里 的 水 是 不 能 用 斗 来 测 量 的，

fēnbiàn yí ge rén de hǎo huài yě bù néng zhǐ yǐ tā
分 辨 一 个 人 的 好 坏 也 不 能 只 以 他

de wàimào lái pànduàn.
的 外 貌 来 判 断。

Zhè tiáo yànyǔ gàosu rénmen: Bù néng guāng yǐ
这 条 谚 语 告 诉 人 们：不 能 光 以

wàibiǎo lái pàndìng yí ge rén de hǎo huài, nàyàng zuò
外 表 来 判 定 一 个 人 的 好 坏，那 样 做

shì huì fàn hěn dà de cuòwu de.
是 会 犯 很 大 的 错 误 的。

A man can't be known by his appearance, nor can the sea be measured with a dipper

People should not be judged by their appearances and the sea can not be measured with a dipper.

This proverb tells us that we shouldn't judge a person only by his

appearance. If we act in that way, we'll make a great mistake.

Ruò yào rén bù zhī, chúfēi jǐ mò wéi
若 要 人 不 知， 除 非 己 莫 为

Yí ge rén zuò shìqing rúguǒ bù xiǎng ràng biérén
一 个 人 做 事 情 如 果 不 想 让 别 人
zhīdao shì bù kěnéng de, chúfēi zìjǐ bú qù zuò tā.
知 道 是 不 可 能 的， 除 非 自 己 不 去 做 它。
Zhè zé yànyǔ zhǐchū, gànle huài shì, chízǎo
这 则 谚 语 指 出， 干 了 坏 事， 迟 早
dōu huì bèi biérén zhīdao de. Tā gàojiè rénmen
都 会 被 别 人 知 道 的。 它 告 诫 人 们
qiānwàn búyào yǐwéi mán de guò biérén jiù kěyǐ
千 万 不 要 以 为 瞒 得 过 别 人 就 可 以
suí xīn suǒ yù.
随 心 所 欲。

There is a witness everywhere

If you don't want others to know what you've done, it is better not to do it in the first place.

The meaning of this proverb is that as long as you did bad things, sooner or later others will know. It warns people that never think you can do whatever pleases you as long as you can cover it up.

Appendix 3

歇后语六则
Xiēhòuyǔ Liù Zé

Six two-part allegorical sayings

矮子爬楼梯——步步登高
Ǎizi pá lóutī —— bù bù dēng gāo

矮个儿的人，每爬一步梯子，就登高一节。再往上爬就更高一节，这就是"步步登高"。

Ǎi gèr de rén, měi pá yí bù tīzi, jiù dēng gāo yì jié. Zài wǎngshàngpá jiù gèng gāo yì jié, zhè jiù shì "bù bù dēng gāo".

这个歇后语通常用来形容官场上的平步青云、地位高升等情况，或指人的生活越来越好，不断提高等。

Zhège xiēhòuyǔ tōngcháng yònglái xíngróng guānchǎng shang de píng bù qīngyún、dìwèi gāoshēng děng qíngkuàng, huò zhǐ rén de shēnghuó yuè lái yuè hǎo, búduàn tígāo děng.

A short person goes up the stairs—ascending step by step

A short person, once he goes up one stair, he ascends one step. He goes up another stair, he ascends higher again. This is called "ascending step by step".

This saying is often used to describe people's rapid promotion in official circles or social status. It is also used to describe that people's lives is becoming better and better.

Chinese Crash Course

Chuānghu shang de zhǐ — yì chuō jiù pò
窗户上的纸——一戳就破

　　Hěn zǎo yǐqián, hái méiyou fāmíng bōli, rénmen
　　很早以前，还没有发明玻璃，人们
jiù yòng hěn báo de zhǐ lái hú chuānghu. Kěshì zhǐ yòu báo
就用很薄的纸来糊窗户。可是纸又薄
yòu ruǎn, zhǐyào yòng shǒu yì chuō jiù pò le.
又软，只要用手一戳就破了。
　　Xiànzài zhège xiēhòuyǔ duō yònglái bǐyù shāo yì
　　现在这个歇后语多用来比喻稍一
zhǐdiǎn jiù míngbai.
指点就明白。

Window paper—torn by a touch

　　Long ago, people used a kind of semi-transparent paper to cover a window in place of glass. They stuck it with paste on windows. But if you poke it with one finger, it would be torn.

　　This saying originally indicates the paper on the window is very flimsy. Now it refers to understanding something quickly only with a few hints.

Dǎkāi tiānchuāng — shuō liàng huà
打开天窗——说亮话

　　Shuōhuà de shíhou dǎkāi tiānchuāng, zhèyàng, guāngxiàn
　　说话的时候打开天窗，这样，光线
gèng liàng le, kàn de gèng qīngchu, shuō chū de huà zìrán
更亮了，看得更清楚，说出的话自然

Appendix 3

jiù shì "liàng huà" le.
就是"亮话"了。

"Dǎkāi tiānchuāng— shuō liàng huà" chángyònglái zhǐ zhíjié
"打开天窗——说亮话"常用来指直截

liǎodàng de bǎ shìqing shuō míngbai. Nǐ búbì bàn zhē bàn
了当地把事情说明白。你不必半遮半

yǎn de, wǒ yě búbì duǒduǒ shǎnshǎn de.
掩的,我也不必躲躲闪闪的。

Opening the skylight—let's be frank

When we are talking with others, we open the skylight. The room will become bright, so the words that we say are blunt ones.

This saying often refers to calling a spade a spade.

Dǎpò shāguō— wèn (wèn) dào dǐ
打破沙锅——问(璺)到底

Shāguō yídàn bèi dǎpò, lièhén jiù jiāng cóng shàng-
沙锅一旦被打破,裂痕就将从上

mian yìzhí liè dào xiàmian. Zhèxiē lièhén chēng "wèn".
面一直裂到下面。这些裂痕称"璺"。

"Wèn" yǔ "wèn" xiéyīn, "wèn dào dǐ" jiù chéngwéi "wèn
"璺"与"问"谐音,"璺到底"就成为"问

dào dǐ".
到底"。

Zhè shì yí ge yùnyòng xiéyīn déchū de xiēhòuyǔ.
这是一个运用谐音得出的歇后语。

Chinese Crash Course

Tā de yìsi shì, wèile xúnzhǎo shìqing de yóulái huò
它 的 意 思 是, 为 了 寻 找 事 情 的 由 来 或
dá'àn, fēi yào wèn ge qīngchu bù kě.
答 案, 非 要 问 个 清 楚 不 可。

Getting to the bottom of a matter

If the earthenware pot breaks, it cracks all the way to the bottom. The cracks are called "璺". "璺" and "问" (ask) are homophones. "Crack to the bottom" can turn into "ask to the bottom".

The meaning of this saying is that in order to look for an answer, one keeps asking questions until he gets to the bottom of it.

Gǒu yǎo Lǚ Dòngbīn —— bù shí hǎorén xīn
狗 咬 吕 洞 宾 —— 不 识 好 人 心

Lǚ Dòngbīn shì mínjiān chuánshuō "bā xiān" zhōng de
吕 洞 宾 是 民 间 传 说 "八 仙" 中 的
yí wèi shénxian, yě shì yí ge xíng xiá zhàng yì de
一 位 神 仙, 也 是 一 个 行 侠 仗 义 的
hǎoxīnrén, tā jīngcháng chéngzhì huàirén bāngzhù qióngrén,
好 心 人, 他 经 常 惩 治 坏 人 帮 助 穷 人,
shēn dé rénjiān bǎixìng chóngjìng. Dànshì gǒu què bú rènshi Lǚ
深 得 人 间 百 姓 崇 敬。 但 是 狗 却 不 认 识 吕
Dòngbīn, bǎ tā dàng huàirén yǎo, suǒyǐ shuō tā "bù shí
洞 宾, 把 他 当 坏 人 咬, 所 以 说 它 "不 识
hǎorénxīn".
好 人 心"。

Rénmen yòng zhège xiēhòuyǔ lái zhǐ hǎo huài bù
人们 用 这个 歇后语 来 指 好 坏 不
fēn, bǎ biéren de hǎoxīn dàngchéng èyì.
分，把 别人 的 好心 当成 恶意。

Snarl and snap at Lü Dongbin—wrong a kind-hearted person

Lü Dongbin was one of the Eight Immortals in Chinese mythology and was a kind-hearted man. He often punished the evil-doers and helped the poor. People respected him very much. But the dog didn't know him, and snarled at and bit him. So this figure of speech means "doesn't know a kind-hearted person".

People use this saying to refer to regarding one's good intention as a bad one.

Hán Xìn yòng bīng — duō duō yì shàn
韩 信 用 兵 —— 多 多 益 善

Hán Xìn shì Hàncháo de yì yuán dà jiàng, tā fēicháng
韩 信 是 汉朝 的 一 员 大 将，他 非常
shànyú dài bīng. Yǒu yí cì Hán Xìn dài bīng chū zhēng, huángdì
擅 于 带 兵。有 一 次 韩 信 带 兵 出 征，皇帝
wèn tā yào dài duōshao bīng, tā shuō: "Dāngrán shì yuè duo yuè
问 他 要 带 多少 兵，他 说："当然 是 越 多 越
hǎo le, zhèyàng cái yǒulì yú zuò zhàn ma."
好 了，这样 才 有利 于 作 战 嘛。"
Hòulái, rénmen jiù yòng "duō duō yi shàn" lái zhǐ
后 来，人们 就 用 "多 多 益 善" 来 指

dōngxi　yuè duō yuè hǎo.
东　西　越　多　越　好。

Like Han Xin commanding troops—the more the better

  Han Xin, a great general in the Han Dynasty, was good at commanding troops. Once, he was ready to command an expedition. The emperor asked him how many soldiers he wanted. He said: "The more troops, the better. This is beneficial to the battle."

  Later, people use this saying to mean the more possession they have, the better.

Appendix 4

典故四则 (Diǎngù Sì Zé)

Four allusions

百闻不如一见 (Bǎi wén bùrú yí jiàn)

西汉宣帝时期,羌人入侵,宣帝派赵充领兵平定。宣帝问他要派多少兵马,赵充说:"听别人说一百遍,不如亲眼看一遍,我要亲自到前线去看一看。"经过亲自观察地形,他清楚了敌人的兵力部署,并制定了详细的用兵计划,很顺利地平定了羌人的侵扰。

"百闻不如一见"指的是听一百次不如亲自见一次。表示听到的再多,也

Chinese Crash Course

bù rú qīn yǎn suǒ jiàn lái de kěkào.
不 如 亲 眼 所 见 来 得 可 靠。

It is better to see once than to hear a hundred times

During the reign of Emperor Xuan in the Western Han Dynasty, the Qiangs invaded the inland. Emperor Xuan sent Zhao Chong to command troops to put down the invaders. The emperor asked him how many troops and horses he would need. Zhao Chong said: "It's better to see once than hear a hundred times. I will go to the front and look it over." He worked out a detailed plan after the inspection. Then he put down the intrusion of the Qiang people successfully.

This story indicates seeing is believing.

Chéng yě Xiāo Hé, bài yě Xiāo Hé
成 也 萧 何, 败 也 萧 何

Hán Xìn yuán zài Xiàng Yǔ jūn zhōng rènzhí, yīnwèi bú shòu
韩 信 原 在 项 羽 军 中 任 职, 因 为 不 受
zhòngyòng, zhuǎn'ér tóubèn dào Liú Bāng jūn zhōng, dàn réng bú bèi
重 用, 转 而 投 奔 到 刘 邦 军 中, 但 仍 不 被
zhòngshì. Liú Bāng shǒuxià de móushì Xiāo Hé fāxiàn Hán Xìn
重 视。 刘 邦 手 下 的 谋 士 萧 何 发 现 韩 信
quèshí shì yí ge nánde de réncái, jiù xiàng Liú Bāng tuī-
确 实 是 一 个 难 得 的 人 才, 就 向 刘 邦 推
jiàn. Dàn Liú Bāng háishi méiyou zhòngyòng tā, Hán Xìn biàn lián
荐。 但 刘 邦 还 是 没 有 重 用 他, 韩 信 便 连

Appendix 4

yè táozǒule. Xiāo Hé dézhī hòu, bǎ tā zhuī huílai, bìng

夜逃走了。萧何得知后，把他追回来，并

ràng Liú Bāng zhòngyòngle tā. Cǐhòu, Hán Xìn lǚ jiàn qí gōng,

让刘邦重用了他。此后，韩信屡建奇功，

wèi Liú Bāng dǎxiàle tiānxià, dàn yě shòudàole Liú Bāng

为刘邦打下了天下，但也受到了刘邦

de cāijì. Hòulái Hán Xìn zhǔnbèi móufǎn, bèi Xiāo Hé hé

的猜忌。后来韩信准备谋反，被萧何和

Lǚ Hòu piànrù huánggōng shāhàile.

吕后骗入皇宫杀害了。

Hòurén yòng "chéng yě Xiāo Hé, bài yě Xiāo Hé" lái biǎo-

后人用"成也萧何，败也萧何"来表

shì mǒu rén mǒu shì de chénggōng hé shībài dōu shì yóu yí

示某人某事的成功和失败都是由一

ge rén zàochéng de.

个人造成的。

Whether success or failure,
it will be caused by Xiao He himself

Han Xin originally held a post in the troops of Xiang Yu. Because he was not given any important position, he went to the troops of Liu Bang. But he also didn't receive adequate attention. Xiao He, one of the wise men of Liu Bang also recommended Han Xin because he found Han Xin was a rare talent. Liu Bang also ignored him, so Han Xin escaped. After Xiao He heard that, he chased him back and let Liu Bang grant him an important position. After that, Han Xin fought many successful battles and helped Liu Bang seize state power. But he was suspected by Liu Bang

because of his overwhelming achievements. Later, Xiao He and Empress Lü beguiled Han Xin into entering the imperial palace and killed him because he was planning to rebel.

Later people use this saying to refer to success and failure of somebody or something are both due to the same person or factor.

Dōng chuāng shì fā
东 窗 事 发

Sòngcháo Qín Huì céng hé qīzi Wáng shì zài dōng chuāng xià
宋 朝 秦 桧 曾 和 妻 子 王 氏 在 东 窗 下
mìmóu shāhàile Yuè Fēi. Qín Huì sǐ hòu, Wáng shì qǐng fāng-
密 谋 杀 害 了 岳 飞。 秦 桧 死 后, 王 氏 请 方
shì zuò fǎ shì, fāngshì dàole yīnjiān, kànjiàn Qín Huì zài
士 做 法 事, 方 士 到 了 阴 间, 看 见 秦 桧 在
shòu xíngfá. Qín Huì duì fāngshì shuō: "Máfan nǐ gěi wǒ
受 刑 罚。 秦 桧 对 方 士 说: "麻 烦 你 给 我
fūren chuán ge kǒuxìn, jiù shuō dōng chuāng xià de shìqing bào-
夫 人 传 个 口 信, 就 说 东 窗 下 的 事 情 暴
lùle."
露 了。"

"Dōngchuāng shì fā" yònglái bǐyù yīnmóu bàilù huò
"东 窗 事 发" 用 来 比 喻 阴 谋 败 露 或
zuìxíng bèi jiēfā.
罪 行 被 揭 发。

Appendix 4

Eastern window plot

Qin Hui of the Song Dynasty and his wife Wang conspired to murder Yue Fei, a patriotic military commander. After Qin Hui died, Wang asked a necromancer to do the religious services. He went to the nether world and saw that Qin Hui was being tortured. Qin Hui said to the necromancer: "Please tell my wife that what we conspired to murder Yue Fei under the eastern window was exposed."

This idiom is a metaphor to describe that a plot or crime comes to light.

Dōng Shān zài qǐ
东 山 再 起

东晋名士谢安,曾担任著作郎,后来觉得当官受约束,便辞官到东山隐居。后来,大司马桓温邀请他出山做官,他答应了,并最终凭借自己的才能做了宰相。

"东山再起"指再度出任官职。后用来比喻失败后重新得势。

To regain power after coming out from the East Mountain
(to bob up like a cork)

Xie An was a famous intellectual in the Eastern Jin Dynasty. He was once the official in charge of literature. But he felt being confined as an official and resigned to live in seclusion in the East Mountain. Later Huan Wen, Minister of War, invited him to work for the court again. He agreed and finally became the prime minister through his own efforts.

This idiom means to resume one's position. It also means to regain one's power after failure.